HAVE YOU:

- *bribed your kids with candy to make it through the supermarket?*
- *forced them to clean their plates to get dessert?*
- *withheld food from "fat" kids?*
- *held your daughter's weight to a different standard than your son's?*
- *asked your pediatrician if your child's weight was "normal"?*

FIT KIDS is your lifesaver. Eileen Behan, a registered dietitian for more than twenty-five years, not only gives parents the facts they need to handle the dicey issue of children and obesity, she releases parents from the stereotypical myths about food and eating that have been uppermost in our minds for decades. *FIT KIDS* provides a sensible and comprehensive diet and activity plan for children and their parents, so they can both enjoy their food and develop good eating habits for the rest of their lives. This book can help your children lose weight, boost their grades, improve self-image, and strengthen family relationships.

FIT KIDS

FIT KIDS

Raising Physically
and Emotionally
Strong Kids
with Real Food

EILEEN BEHAN, R.D.

POCKET BOOKS
New York   London   Toronto   Sydney   Singapore

The author of this book is not a physician, and the ideas, procedures, and suggestions in this book are not intended as a substitute for the medical advice of a trained health professional. All matters regarding your health require medical supervision. Consult your physician before adopting the suggestions in this book, as well as about any condition that may require diagnosis or medical attention. The author and publisher disclaim any liability arising directly or indirectly from the use of this book.

An *Original* Publication of POCKET BOOKS

 POCKET BOOKS, a division of Simon & Schuster, Inc.
1230 Avenue of the Americas, New York, NY 10020

Copyright © 2001 by Eileen Behan

All rights reserved, including the right to reproduce this book or portions thereof in any form whatsoever. For information address Pocket Books, 1230 Avenue of the Americas, New York, NY 10020

Behan, Eileen.
    Fit kids : raising physically and emotionally strong kids with real food / Eileen Behan.
        p. cm.
    Includes bibliographical references and index.
    ISBN 0-671-03716-1
    1. Children—Nutrition.   2. Diet therapy for children.   I. Title.
RJ206.B447 2001   00-68215

First Pocket Books trade paperback printing May 2001

10 9 8 7 6 5 4 3 2 1

POCKET and colophon are registered trademarks of Simon & Schuster, Inc.

Cover design by Regina Starace
Photo credits: PictureQuest, Tony Stone Images, Siede Preis/Photodisc

Printed in the U.S.A.

To David

Without your support this book could never have been written.

Acknowledgments

So many people help in the writing of a book. Trish Cronan and Brad Lavigne, thank you for your encouragement and support. Sharon, Sheila, and Elizabeth Behan, your enthusiasm for my projects is always needed. Madeleine Walsh, Judith Paige, and Marilyn DeSimone, I always welcome and need your frank and honest comments. Sarah and Emily, you make everything worthwhile.

I would like to thank Tracy Sherrod for her excellence as an editor. I am very grateful she understood the importance and scope of this subject. Also at Pocket Books I would like to thank Emily Bestler for her continued support, and Ronald Taylor, who made the publication process easier. Special thanks to Carol Mann. Most of all I would like to acknowledge the scientists who publish their research about nutrition, behavior, and eating patterns. Without their work there would be no recommendations to make.

Contents

Introduction

In the late 1990s I began working on a book I would never write called *The Power of Food in the Family*. In it, I intended to make the case that food can be a means to strengthen families. Mary Pipher writes in her book *Reviving Ophelia* about how our young people move in a world of strangers, no longer nurtured by a cohesive community, and as a result they feel isolated and vulnerable. She is not alone in her observation or concern. As a nutritionist I certainly have heard parallel worries from clients who complain about harried schedules that squeeze family time almost into nonexistence. They tell me they are stressed and worry that their children are unhappy too. I believe that the way a family buys, prepares, and serves food can help alleviate these problems.

I am not objective about the power of food and its pleasures. Food is my work, and cooking is my hobby. It's what I do when I want to celebrate, and it's one of the ways I connect with my children, husband, and friends. To a psychologist this might sound misguided, but enjoying food is not synonymous with obsession, emotional bankruptcy, or a means to elicit affection. Food used correctly can make children feel strong and confident. Returning to old-fashioned food basics such as cooking and eating together can be an effective tool to help parents raise healthy, strong, enthusiastic children in a culture that some mental health experts define as toxic because of its emphasis on commercialism and self-gratification. The problem with the book I started was that I couldn't make a good enough case for why families should take a different approach to how they handled food within the family. Everyone readily agrees that good nutrition is important and that food is the conveyor of nutrition. What does it then matter when, where, or how we eat, as long as we eat enough and not too much?

In the fall of 1998, the United States Department of Agriculture and the U.S. surgeon general convened a panel of obesity experts to examine and comment on the current status of obesity among our children. The results were shocking: one in five of our children is now considered overweight or obese, up fifty percent in the past twenty years, and all evidence suggests the number is climbing, not stagnant. Because I specialize in family nutrition I was asked to write this book to tell parents how to help their child lose weight. I have written five books related to children and health and I have two daughters, aged eleven and thirteen, which gives me a valuable perspective when writing about children and food. I have also been a practicing nutritionist for over twenty-five years, working with individuals, children, and families to use food to improve health.

The one good thing about the obesity crisis is it clearly identifies something has gone very wrong with our food supply, our children's health, and how we as a nation think of food and children. In the past decade as I raised my own children I have seen and had to navigate a food supply that has been altered dramatically since I was a child. Our shelves are filled with empty-calorie food that in many cases is falsely marketed to parents as being nutritious with words like *lite, fat free,* and *contains real fruit.* I am convinced, and many experts agree, that this new food environment is the reason we have a childhood obesity epidemic. The change in our food supply and family food traditions may also explain why some young people feel disconnected from their community. Parents may be surprised to learn that a YMCA parent and teen survey found the top concern among teenagers was not having enough time together with their parents. In a White House report by the Council of Economic Advisers, teens who eat dinner with their parents five times per week were less likely to smoke, drink, use drugs, or be involved in violence or early sexual activity. Kids who ate with their parents had a lower incidence of suicide attempts and better grades. For centuries human beings have gathered together to share food, whether it was around an open fire or a family table, but today we do not need to do this. The introduction of the microwave and other conveniences makes it possible to eat in isolation at any time. The changes brought about by two-parent work-ing families make it harder to eat relaxed family meals together. In a professional journal called *Family Networker Magazine*, one psychotherapist describes assigning eating family meals together as homework for her clients as a way to get them reconnected.

As I read through my old notes about the power of food, this time with an eye on focusing the material on how to treat childhood obesity, I knew I had to find a way for parents to make meals and food enjoyable and pleasurable even when a child is overweight. It also became clear to me that not only the overweight child deserves the family's attention in this area, but also all siblings (old and young), and Mom and Dad too. Food is an issue not just for the overweight but for anyone who wants to live a long, healthful life.

The obesity epidemic is the white elephant in the room. This rise in obesity has occurred not because of

hormones or genetic makeup but because we have created an environment for our children that is unhealthy.
Parents need to protect their children from this environment because it will cause them to overeat, and they need
to protect them from the advertising messages that tell
them life will be better if they EAT, EAT, EAT. Do not
feel hopeless if your child is overweight. Children can be
successful at losing weight when they have the help and
support of the family. In a study, seventy-six children
were divided into three groups, all receiving similar diet
and exercise advice. One group monitored only the child,
another only attendance, but in the third group the parent and child worked together. It was the latter group that
had the most success, which persisted even at five- and
ten-year follow-ups. Children also have the advantage of
being young; their eating habits are not entrenched.

In this book I will ask families to rethink what they
know about losing weight and ask parents to evaluate
what food means in their family. I am not recommending
a diet that restricts or deprives, I am asking for the opposite. I am asking the family to provide a menu of delicious,
good-tasting food, with regularity and variety. I am asking
that you examine the role food plays in your family. Is it
punishment? Is it a reward? How do you speak about
food? I am suggesting to families that being more
thoughtful about what and when you feed your child will
not only help him reach a weight that is appropriate for
his age and height but will also strengthen your relationship. You will make your child feel secure and confident,
loved and cared for. You will use the power of food to
help your child and your family be the best it can be, and
you can start at your very next meal.

The goal of this book is to provide parents with tools

they will need to guide their child to natural, gradual weight loss. These tools consist of knowing not only the facts about weight loss, but also what leads to success and what leads to failure. Parents need to look at their style of parenting to examine if it contributes to a child being overweight. The role of exercise is essential for a child to reach his natural weight and to help him feel good about himself. Eating a menu of real, minimally processed foods as a way to control weight and appetite will be emphasized. To make eating such a menu practical I have created the Real Food Diet. This is a system that categorizes food into Everyday, Sometime, and Occasional food choices. You and your child decide what to eat, with two important qualifications: three organized meals every day, and each family member must eat or at least taste the recommended servings from each food group on most days. Children are in charge of how much they eat, and parents are in charge of the food purchased and prepared.

My approach requires that your child and the whole family become more conscientious about what you choose to eat. Don't be surprised if you see secondary benefits from the Real Food Diet that include a strengthened relationship and a blossoming of your child's sense of self-worth. It is all possible because of the power of food.

FIT KIDS

1

≡

Is My Child Overweight?

I was shocked that some girls in my class wanted to know about fat versus muscle, how do you lose fat, what is anorexia, bulimia, etc.

—GRADE FOUR ELEMENTARY SCHOOL TEACHER

At the end of the year we all wanted to take pictures, at least the kids with cameras did, but Betsy wouldn't let us because she said pictures make her look fat.

—FIFTH-GRADE STUDENT

What and how you feed your family is an important issue for every child, no matter what their weight. Being overweight is a potentially serious health problem, but the overweight child who obtains family support, adopts a healthy style of eating, and exercises will be healthier than the normal weight child who does not receive such intervention. A recent survey of over three thousand American children found that the number of servings these children were eating from the recommended food groups was below the recommended level for every food group except in the dairy group, and only one percent of the children met all food group recommendations. A 1999 report in the *Journal of the American Medical Association* found that the buildup of fatty plaques that can lead to heart disease begins in childhood, and the authors suggest that a better diet in childhood or adolescence is needed for prevention. This research, as well as the trend in weight gain among our children, suggests that an improved menu can be beneficial and prevent disease for all children, whether lean or fat.

WHY ARE SO MANY AMERICAN KIDS OVERWEIGHT?

The number of kids who are considered obese is so great that an obesity epidemic has been declared by health professionals. Depending on whose survey you examine it is estimated that 25 to 30 percent of our children are considered obese. The prevalence in obesity has increased by 54 percent in children six to eleven years of age, and 39 percent in adolescents twelve to seventeen years of age. Most of this weight gain has occurred since the late 1970s. Between the time of the first National Health and Nutrition Examination Survey (NHANES) in 1976 to 1980 and its repeat in 1988 to 1991 the prevalence of obesity increased by approximately 40 percent. Hispanic, Native American, and black children tend to be affected the most, but the spread of obesity among all children continues to increase rapidly—so much so that today's clothing manufacturers are expanding their line of "husky" sizes to meet demand.

The age of puberty is now at 12.8 years of age, while a century ago it was at 15 or 16 years of age. Most researchers believe that a child's percentage of body fat influences the onset of puberty more than chronological age and that the earlier onset reflects the availability of food and the increase in body fat among our children. But not only our kids are gaining weight; in the first NHANES survey 24 percent of adults were obese, but by the third survey that number increased to 33 percent. One survey has found that half of all adults are considered overweight. A 1999 *Boston Globe* article reported that adults have gained so much weight, many can't fit into commercial seats anymore. Seating standards developed in the 1950s allowed eighteen inches to accommodate the average backside, whereas today's stadium seats are being refitted to add an extra four inches and airlines are lifting tray tables to accommodate bigger tummies.

Such significant and dramatic weight increases over a single decade cannot be explained by genetic causes. Dr. Michael Rosenbaum from the Department of Pediatrics, College of Physicians and Surgeons at Columbia University in New York, has written that "the rapid increase in the prevalence of obesity emphasizes the role of environmental factors, because genetics could not occur at this rate." These environmental factors include low activity levels and the wide availability of food.

IS YOUR CHILD OVERWEIGHT?

To address the problem of your child's weight, you first have to assess whether your child really is overweight, and then you have to understand how and why it happened, and what to do about it. Most of us think we can recognize when someone is overweight. But can we? As parents we are not objective about our children, and we bring our fears and experience to every situation, which colors our perception: for example, a mother with a history of weight problems may interpret her son's natural chubbiness as obesity. A father who has never had a weight issue may not recognize that his daughter's weight gain is above what is considered normal.

Parents may put adult body standards on children. This doesn't work, because body proportions are different. Ask your child to put a hand over his head so the elbow faces out. Note where the elbow is in relationship to the top of the head. Now you do the same exercise. In adults, the elbow meets the top of the head, but kids naturally have shorter arms and legs, in proportion to their heads, than adults do, making adult body ideals impossible for kids.

Because parents can't be objective and are not trained in normal childhood growth patterns, you must involve your doctor in answering your concerns about your child's weight. A physician will take into consideration age, growth, and the overall trend in height and weight development. Children grow at unpredictable rates. It is possible for a child to put on weight and "grow into" it a year later. Your doctor can put your child's rate of growth into an appropriate perspective.

You may want to talk about your child's weight to your child's doctor in private or over the phone, not because this is a secretive or taboo subject but because a child may interpret the conversation in a way that says something is wrong with him. The issue of weight can be very emotional, and even young children know that being overweight is socially unacceptable. Your doctor may be skilled at diagnosing a medical problem, but not all doctors or health care workers are aware of how emotional the issue of weight can be. A casual remark such as "You better eat less" or "You're getting a little chubby" can actually sow the seeds for disordered eating. In relation to food, always keep the emphasis on health and not on appearance or whether your child has been "good" or "bad." You'll read more about talking to your child about weight in chapters 3, 7, and 9.

Traditionally a physician will use the National Center for Health Statistic (NCHS) Percentiles to track your child's growth. As of June 2000 the Centers for Disease Control and Prevention have made revised growth charts available to health care providers. The new charts reflect the nation's cultural and racial diversity. Childhood obesity is defined in an American Heart Association statement as a weight for height above the seventy-fifth percentile for age and sex. A child who has significantly increased his weight for height and suffers from a medical condition that can be exacerbated by excessive weight gain, such as high cholesterol levels, diabetes, or high blood pressure, may also be considered obese. The physician's weight charts are helpful, but don't be a slave to them; just a few pounds can put a child into a higher or lower weight percentile.

In addition to the standard height and weight percentile your doctor may evaluate your child's body mass index (BMI). This is your child's weight in kilograms divided by height in meters squared. The BMI is recommended as a way to screen for obesity because it correlates both subcutaneous fat and total body fatness. Obesity by definition occurs when the body has excess fat tissue. It is possible for a child (and even an adult) to be over-

weight without being overfat. A child is considered overweight if his BMI is equal to or in excess of the ninety-
fifth percentile for age and gender or greater than a BMI
of 30. If your child is heavier than 85 percent of children
who are the same age and height your child is considered
overweight. See page 264 in chapter 9 for more information about BMI. The doctor will pay specific attention to
the relationship between the increase in weight to
height.

Prepubescent growth, "plumpness," which is a natural
occurrence starting at age eight in girls and ten in boys, is
often the cause for concern in parents, but as the adolescent growth spurt approaches, usually by age eleven,
changes occur in height too. During this time kids require
calories and nutrition to meet their growth needs. Again,
rely on your health care team to interpret weight and
growth trends.

During a routine visit your medical provider can easily determine your child's weight and height and provide
advice on how to interpret it. Do not rely on your home
scale to evaluate your child's weight. The scale may not
be accurate, and it doesn't take into account your child's
rate of growth. If you encourage your child to check her
weight on the home scale for the purpose of evaluating
her "progress," you will have introduced her to a practice
capable of undermining her self-esteem and sabotaging
good health behaviors in the future. The scale should be
used as a medical tool, just like a blood pressure cuff or a
stethoscope, neither of which you would use on your
child with any regularity at home, so don't do the same
with the scale. Using a scale suggests that it measures
dieting success. But a change in weight does not necessar-
ily indicate a shift in body fat or that a child's health is

improving. Body fluids, muscle growth, bone development, even the last meal will all influence body weight. If you want to do something helpful for your family, then deemphasize the scale. By age eight or ten many children will see the scale as a measurement of their self-worth. When the scale holds a prominent space in the bathroom or if a child sees a parent checking weight regularly, then your child will learn that the scale is important. The scale is not important! It does not measure the habits that will actually lead your child to his or her natural weight.

A doctor's evaluation is needed to establish if a child is obese and to help determine its cause. If your child is overweight your doctor will assess his risk for cardiac disease, weight-related orthopedic problems, and psychological or emotional issues. Overweight children tend to have higher cholesterol levels, higher blood pressure, even more skin disorders.

CAN HORMONES BE THE CAUSE OF MY CHILD'S WEIGHT GAIN?

In only a small number of cases will hormones or other genetic factors be the cause of your child's weight gain. However, it is important to rule out a genetic or hormonal defect. This can be done with a careful medical history and physical exam. Children with genetic or hormonal causes of obesity are not only fatter than their peers, but they are also usually shorter, often below the fifth percentile for height for their age. In contrast, children with obesity caused by lifestyle and environment are usually tall (above fiftieth percentile for their age) but otherwise have a normal physical exam, and they often have a family history of obesity. Children with obesity as a consequence of a medical problem often do not have a family history of obesity.

Hypothyroidism is probably the most often cited cause of obesity, though in truth it is rarely encountered. If hypothyroidism is suspected the doctor can measure TSH (thyroid-stimulating hormone) to diagnose it. In addition to weight gain, hypothyroidism often includes symptoms such as constipation, cold intolerance, and dry skin. Cushing's syndrome is another frequently suspected cause of obesity. Cushing's syndrome is a rare condition occurring when too much cortisol, a hormone, is in the blood. The accumulation of body fat is one of its symptoms. A 24-hour urine test can rule it out.

Is Your Child Ruled by Hunger or Appetite?

Hunger and appetite are the sensations that make eating pleasurable. These are good things; without them your child would lose interest in food and not eat enough to maintain health. And it is satiety or the sensation of fullness that tells your child to stop eating. Hunger is a physical sensation that is unpleasant and occurs in response to changes in the stomach and in blood levels of sugar, insulin, and fatty acids. The sensation of hunger is believed to be controlled by the hypothalmus, which is located in the brain, above the spinal cord. It determines the need for more nutrition and creates the sensation of hunger.

After eating, a feeling of fullness called satiety prompts us to stop eating. Satiety occurs when food accumulates in the stomach and passes into the intestines. Hormones in the digestive track are released, and nerves in the intestines send messages to the brain, where the hypothalamus sorts these signals. Once satiety occurs then the need for eating stops. Satiety is not ruled by the nutritional quality of food. For example, 150 calories of soda has the satiety effect of 150 calories of juice or milk without the benefit of the vitamins, protein, or minerals in the latter. So it is possible to feel full and not be well nourished. You'll read later on that several studies find that food quality can effect satiety and appetite—for example, salty, sweet, and refined foods may cause children to overeat; foods carrying fiber may cause children to eat less.

Appetite is the learned psychological response to food. It is pleasant and can override the absence of hunger. A child may have eaten a meal and feel full or satiated, but when presented with a desirable food such as a slice of pie or warm french fries his appetite will allow him to eat more. In other circumstances a child may be hungry but lose his appetite because of an unpleasant psychological experience such as jitters about the first day of school.

If your child is eating because of appetite and not hunger you want to help him distinguish between the two sensations. This is not as hard as you might think. It requires that there be a meal structure in place, and an emphasis on whole foods that naturally control appetite. Your child (and the whole family) is living in a food environment that is unique in all of history and that is causing us to overeat based on appetite and not hunger. For the first time a society has an abundance of good-tasting, inexpensive, widely available, and heavily marketed food. We have an appetite for such foods and eat them whether we are hungry or not. This wide availability of food coincides with a reduction in serious gastrointestinal infections that

increased energy needs, a lower breast-feeding rate
(breast-feeding may help babies learn independent hunger
regulation), an early introduction of solid foods to babies,
which may thwart hunger regulation, the almost national
availability of school lunch programs, and equally important, a reduced opportunity for exercise.

How Does a Child Lose and Gain Weight?

Simply put, children (and adults) gain weight when
energy intake is greater than energy output, that is, we eat
more than we actually need. When excess food is consumed the extra calories are stored as fat. The human
body is capable of storing enormous amounts of energy in
the form of fat cells. When children gain weight they
increase fat cell size as well as the number of fat cells,
whereas grown-ups with adult onset obesity increase the
size of their fat cells but not their number.

The role of activity in weight gain may be just as
important as food. Obese children may not eat more than
their peers, but they may be less active. Writing in the
journal *American Family Physician*, Dr. Rebecca Moran
refers to several studies finding that obese children do not
consume significantly more calories than their thin peers.
In theory it takes 3,500 calories to yield one pound of
body fat. If a child eats an extra 50 to 100 calories above
what he needs in a day (and that can be consumed in one
granola bar or a cookie) that could add up to an extra five
to ten pounds over a year. Or if a child comes home from
school and watches TV instead of playing basketball or
takes the bus to school instead of walking, he has missed
the opportunity to burn a few extra calories. Just a modest
imbalance in food and exercise can lead to a slow, consistent

weight gain. Such an imbalance is likely to be the major explanation behind our current obesity epidemic, which means that the overweight child may eat too much, exercise too little, or a combination of the two.

DOES OBESITY HAVE TO RUN IN FAMILIES?

We can't deny our family biology. Just as we inherit eye color, personality characteristics, and even physical mannerisms, we also inherit our body type. Studies of twins, adoptees, and families find that body weight is as much influenced by our genetic makeup as is our potential for height. The weights of identical twins raised in separate households are very similar, suggesting quite strongly that genes do play a role in what we will weigh.

However it is hard to separate the environment from the genetic; skinfold tests between children and parents living together correlate closely. When parents are divided into body fat classifications of lean, medium, or obese their children increase in fatness as their parent combination increases in fatness, and an overweight child under three years of age does not predict future obesity unless one of the child's parents is also obese. This suggests a genetic component to being overweight, but it might also mean that in a household with one overweight parent foods may be more plentiful or prepared with more calories. Given that the weight of our children is increasing while the gene pool remains relatively constant, it is more likely the parents' food decisions that affect the weight of a child rather than the genes the child inherits. Genetics do play a role in what your child weighs, but the current rise in obesity cannot be explained simply by a genetic propensity toward obesity. Otherwise we would have been overweight all along; instead our kids are getting fatter because of the environment we have created for them. The good news is that environment is something we can change.

Why Is It So Difficult to Lose Weight?

It is assumed that the human body's ability to store energy as fat has ensured its survival and improved its ability to reproduce. Humans are probably equipped with genes that promote energy intake and minimize energy expenditure. However, the calorically dense food and sedentary lifestyle of today's environment result in our genes working against us. Such evolutionary controls are probably the reason adults have a very difficult time losing weight and keeping it off. It is estimated that 90 percent to 95 percent of adults who lose weight return to their previous weight. Part of this regain may be the way that the body compensates by lowering calorie requirements once weight is lost. For example, more calories are burned by the woman who weighs two hundred pounds than by the woman weighting 150 pounds, walking at the same pace. Another reason adults have so much trouble is what I call the "six-week-diet trap." Foolishly adults think they can adhere to a diet prescription for a limited time, melt the fat off, and then return to their old ways; obviously such an approach doesn't work, which is why the weight regain statistics are so awful for adults.

The good news for children is that most parents don't like to put their kids on crash, temporary diets. Most parents seem to recognize that kids need good nutrition to maintain their health. And while a parent may not tend to his or her own health needs, I have found when it comes to the child's health, a parent will do whatever it takes to keep the child healthy. It is not known if kids can beat the trap of their elders, but aggressive treatment in childhood may be accompanied by a permanent resetting of the regulatory system that affects weight control. Children may have better prospects than their parents because to maintain weight, adults can eat only enough food to match their energy output, but in the growing child, food intake must exceed what they use in exercise, because they have to eat more to meet their need for growth.

Will My Child Always Be Overweight?

Obesity does tend to track throughout life if ignored. The statistics about weight and children are not good and are similar to those of adults. Studies find that 80 to 90 percent of children return to their weight percentile. Thirty percent of overweight adults became overweight when they were children, and 80 percent of obese adolescents become obese adults. But parents of very young children do not need to panic. These dismal numbers may be due to children following diets that are unworkable and offer only a short-term fix. Research finds that your child's success will increase when there is strong support and parents are actively involved in the effort. The interventions that have been most successful with children were started between ages six and twelve. The healthiest approach is slow weight loss, with an emphasis on reasonable activity and a low-fat diet. Weight gain can be permanent if not treated, but a child's weight is not the only issue. The child who is unnaturally overweight has not only the health problems linked with being overweight but also those that come from eating a poor diet itself, and this includes the increase risk for serious disease in adulthood.

Is It Really Unhealthy for My Child to Be Overweight?

Overweight children are more likely to have high levels of LDL (low-density lipoprotein or "bad") cholesterol, higher levels of triglycerides, and lower levels of HDL (high-density or "good") cholesterol than children who are not overweight. This ratio of blood lipids can increase the risk of heart disease, and as mentioned earlier, research in the *Journal of the American Medical Association* finds atherosclerosis begins in youth. Another serious illness directly linked to weight is diabetes mellitus. In an editorial in *American Family Physician*, Dr. Dennis Styne of the University of California writes that type 2 diabetes mellitus, the type of diabetes most associated with obesity, is now the most common type of diabetes identified at several pediatric diabetes centers. High blood pressure is another medical condition linked to body weight. In childhood, high blood pressure is uncommon, but persistently elevated blood pressure can occur approximately nine times more frequently in the obese child.

Sleep apnea is a sleep disorder characterized by pauses in breathing during sleep, loud snoring, daytime drowsiness, poor school performance, and bed-wetting. This condition may occur in as many as 7 percent of obese children, and in the severely obese child it may be much higher, closer to 30 percent.

Overweight children can have trouble with bone development because the strength of bones and cartilage is designed to carry a certain range of weight. When a child weighs too much the weight may cause a bowing of the leg bones, weakening the bone structure and causing weak, painful knees that limit mobility and prevent activity.

All these problems are the physical consequences of excess weight, and they should be diagnosed and treated by a physician. The consequences that are most heartbreaking to parents are the social and emotional fallout associated with being overweight. Dr. William Dietz, recognized as a leading authority on childhood obesity, writes in the journal *Pediatrics* that "the most widespread consequences of obesity are psychosocial." He reports that children who are overweight are often taller and perceived as being older than their peers, which can lead to inappropriate expectations of the child by adults and disappointment when those expectations can't be met. An overweight child may choose younger children as friends because they are less judgmental about weight. Researchers gave elementary age children a stack of photos of children with a variety of disabilities and different ethnic backgrounds and asked the children to rate the photos from least to most desirable. The children consistently ranked the picture of the overweight child as the least desirable to be a potential friend. As early as ages six and ten, children will associate obesity with the characteristics of being lazy and sloppy.

In a study that followed girls applying to elite New England colleges it was found that those girls who were overweight had a lower acceptance rate than normal-weight girls with similar credentials. In a 1993 survey of ten thousand individuals sixteen to twenty-four years of age called the National Longitudinal Survey of Youth, the effect obesity had on social achievement early in adulthood was examined. The obese young women in this survey completed less advanced education, had a lower family income, a lower rate of marriage, and poverty rates were higher. This trend was found only in the women but not among the men in the survey.

Clearly the trend among our population of children to gain weight has serious physical and emotional repercussions. However, do not respond to your child's weight problem with the knee-jerk reaction of controlling her diet or restricting food. Some of the lower achievement seen among the women in the National Longitudinal Survey could have been due to a lower sense of self-worth brought on by well-meaning parents who focused on weight and not accomplishment. The truth is you cannot control how fat or thin your child is. You only have control over the relationship you create with your child, how food is treated in the home, and the role physical activity plays in your home.

How Is Obesity Treated?

Medical journals describe treatments of obesity as being expensive, lengthy, and generally ineffective. A review of pediatric resident physicians found that many physicians do not address childhood obesity, perhaps because of a feeling of hopelessness (the statistics on successful weight loss are disheartening) or because of an expectation that children will outgrow their chubbiness. Or perhaps they fear that bringing it up will stigmatize or damage a child's self-esteem. Parents might follow their own physician's lead, even when they suspect a problem. I know one parent who felt her son was overweight and eating poorly, but her doctor never brought up the issue of food or nutrition so she assumed it wasn't really a health issue. I know of another family told by their doctor to "cut back" or "try putting your child on a diet" but not given any type of plan. I heard an Emmy Award–winning television actress tell of how her parents and physician created an elaborate "contract" that tied prizes to weight loss but provided no realistic way to ever reach those weight-loss goals.

You might think that the treatment of obesity is simple—put the child on a diet. But conventional "diets" don't work for children and have the potential to truly damage the relationship between parent and child. To treat a weight problem the focus must always be on health. Treatment includes: a good diet with the food and nutrients that will make a child strong and naturally help control appetite to reach natural weight. Such a diet must include some of your child's favorite foods, and it must include regular activity and family support.

Can My Child Take Weight-Loss Medication?

The U.S. Food and Drug Administration has not approved any weight-loss medications for children, and there are no surgical procedures appropriate for children.

How Much Weight Should My Child Lose?

Your focus should be not on weight loss but on the maintenance of normal growth. The overweight child can focus on preventing weight gain, because most children can accomplish this. Some doctors will suggest setting small weight-loss goals—such as five to ten pounds total or one to four pounds per month—so the child does not become overwhelmed or discouraged. Goals like these are best set by a physician as safety net goals. They sound innocent, but when a goal is not met it can create a huge sense of failure for your child. Weight-loss goals do not measure the quality of the food being eaten or the amount of exercise. I have known many adults who lost weight by quick weight-loss methods to meet a weight-loss goal only to regain their weight when they stopped the "diet." Do not encourage your child to follow that path; not only will it fail to produce a natural weight loss but it can also produce poor nutrition and poor performance in your child. Instead of focusing on pounds of weight to be lost, set a goal that includes proper food and regular activity.

WHAT IS NATURAL WEIGHT?

In this book you will hear me refer over and over to your child's natural weight. Natural weight is the weight a child should reach if he is eating a balance of food that meets both energy and growth requirements. It is not a specific number but a level that is determined by healthy eating and exercise habits. Unnatural weight is the level of weight that exists when children are not in balance, and it can indicate that a child is either underweight or overweight. Being underweight can occur when food is scarce or when a child does not recognize the cues to eat, or in the case of being overweight, the environment interferes with the internal system that tells children to stop eating. Your child's natural weight is determined completely by your child's body and it may not abide by the weight percentile charts or our culture's idea of what is ideal.

Don't Overdo It!

Does the natural body weight of a healthy child scare you? The only way to bind these anxieties is with a dose of reality. Ask your doctor for an objective assessment of your child's weight before making any menu changes. In 1987 a New York doctor, Michael T. Pugliese, discovered seven cases of malnutrition caused by well-meaning parents. These parents feared their young children (all under two years of age) might develop health problems on a conventional diet. So in an effort to prevent heart disease and obesity, they cut back on calories and fat by diluting formula, restricting food and snacks, and serving low-fat milk. Fortunately the children all regained health once their parents reinstated a more conventional menu. Don't put your child on a well-intended but overly restricted diet; you may harm him physically and emotionally.

But Don't Ignore the Problem Either

In the preschool and elementary years kids may not be aware of their weight because most of their self-image comes directly from their parents' feedback. Starting in the later elementary school and preadolescent years a child's self-identity and how they perceive themselves is influenced more and more by their peers. This is when children start to devalue themselves because of weight. I am not recommending that you abide by the culture's definition of beauty, which suggests the Barbie doll look to be ideal, but I am recommending that you help your child focus on fitness and health with the goal of reaching her natural and true weight—whatever that might be. As I said earlier, we are living in a unique food environment,

and your children are being marketed foods that will
cause them to overeat. Your family may have slipped into
a lifestyle that allows appetite to dictate food choices. I
am asking you to take a look at what you have created in
your home with regard to food and put the emphasis on
health and fitness. This is an achievable goal that can be
very rewarding. This is not punishment; it is a demonstration of love and responsible parenting. When a parent
pays attention to the quality of what their child eats and
sets goals that include the enjoyment of good food, they
not only give their child the best chance at good health,
but they also promote a positive relationship between
parent and child and they send a message of love and self-
worth. If the doctor says your child is overweight do not
feel guilty about your child's weight. Instead use your
concern to promote good health.

2

≡

The Truth About Diets

Dieting is like trying to breathe through a straw; eventually a person must give up and gasp for air.

—J. P. FOREYT AND G. K. GOODRICK

Our obsession with dieting is a cultural sickness. It induces eating patterns that deprive people of their ability to naturally regulate themselves.

—LAURA FRASER

In 1992 the National Institutes of Health held a conference on how to treat and prevent obesity. It concluded that restrictive diets have only a temporary effect on weight loss. Restrictive diets are menus that limit food choices and restrain calories to a level that is below what is needed by the body. These diets do not work over time for many reasons, including physical and emotional causes. Physically, a restrictive diet will cause changes in fatty acid production, increased fuel mobilization, lower energy expenditure, increased fat storage, and increased energy efficiency. The result is that such diets have the exact opposite effect of what the dieter intended to accomplish, and a calorie-restricted diet often precedes binge eating. Emotionally, a restrictive diet can't work because the focus is on the negative, what should be avoided, and not on the positive, what to include. There is no long-term joy in this type of eating, and within a week or two it becomes too burdensome to continue.

Most dieters believe that if only they had a little more willpower the diet would work for them. The belief in restrictive dieting is promoted again and again in magazines, television advertising, and, most powerful of all, personal testimonials. In testimonials, individuals cite success with their diet and recommend it for others. In the first days and weeks a restrictive diet may look successful. Dieters are usually enthusiastic, feel good, and the accompanying weight loss "proves" that dieting works. Unfortunately in 95 percent of the cases, caloric restriction, monotony, and the preoccupation required to maintain a restrictive diet will lead to relapse, uncontrolled eating, and almost always an overwhelming sense of failure. If you have ever "dieted" or if you are a habitual "dieter" now, do you really want to pass this habit along to your child?

Keep in mind that Americans spend $35 billion on weight reduction products, diet foods, and drinks. There are so many diet books on the market that no single bookstore could carry them all. And yet Americans are getting fatter and fatter and are generally feeling pretty bad about how much their bodies weigh.

If your child is subjected to this type of restrictive dieting, not only will she fail to lose weight, but her self-esteem can also be damaged and her sense of self-worth may plummet. Overall, restrictive dieting is a demeaning process that may sow the seeds for an eating disorder. Even if your child has short-term success with a restrictive diet the odds are against him that he will be able to keep the weight off, and you will have introduced him to what could be a lifelong pattern of unsuccessful and disheartening dieting.

This is not to say that people cannot lose weight. Dr. Rena Wing, professor of psychiatry, psychology, and epidemiology and the director of the Obesity Nutrition Research Center at the University of Pittsburgh, has created a registry of people who have lost at least thirty pounds and kept it off for one year. Almost all of these two thousand individuals say they had to change both eating and activity habits to lose weight and keep it off. Most follow a low-fat diet, eat five times per day, and exercise at a level equal to walking three to four miles daily. This registry is made up of adults, but the point is that weight loss is possible through sensible eating and exercise. This is the message you must pass along to your child. Another significant factor about the participants in the registry is that they report a high level of personal happiness, living a "diet" has not been misery for them but has been satisfying. The same can be true for your child. A child who eats good food and exercises regularly will feel very good about himself, physically and emotionally.

MYTHS ABOUT WEIGHT LOSS

If you want to help your child with weight you must provide her with accurate information. You would not send your child to school believing that the seas are ruled by Poseidon or that the god Apollo makes the sun appear each morning and disappear each night. Yet when it comes to weight loss there is an enormous amount of misinformation that gets repeated again and again. Here are some of the more familiar weight-loss myths and recurring fads that you do not want to pass along to your child as fact. In chapter 9 you will find additional resources about health and food.

Grapefruit Burns Fat

Eating more grapefruit is a good way to increase fruit consumption, but it is no more effective at helping with weight loss than eating any other type of fruit. Contrary to what some diet plans promote, grapefruit does not melt body fat or contain enzymes that burn fat. Tablets of grapefruit concentrate are ineffective too.

The Shrinking Stomach

The stomach is a muscular pouch that has the important job of digesting food and sending it along to the small intestine for absorption. The stomach does "inflate" after a meal and "deflate" when food is digested and moved along the digestive tract, but the stomach cannot shrink any more than a healthy liver or kidney can. When food consumption patterns are changed you can train yourself to feel less hungry at a particular time, but this is due to a change in appetite, not because the stomach actually has decreased in size.

Toast Versus Bread

This is not so widely cited today but patients use to tell me they toasted their bread as a way to cut back on calories. Toasting removes moisture but does not burn calories.

Bread Is Fattening

Bread has a very small amount of total fat. Most of the calories it carries come from carbohydrate, followed by protein, then fat. But what you put on bread can be fattening. Butter and peanut butter or cheese are all high-fat foods. In and of itself bread is not fattening, but when eaten in excess the carbohydrate calories can be stored as fat. The issue is eating more food than you require, not the fact that the calories come from bread.

Low-Carbohydrate Diets

Low-carbohydrate diets are attractive because they can produce dramatic, short-term weight loss. The body goes into a fasting state, using glycogen (stored sugar) as fuel and turning to protein when the glycogen is used up. A dieter may be able to lose seven pounds in two days. A pound or two may be fat, but the remaining five pounds is lean body tissue, water, and minerals. A return to normal eating can replenish lost fluids and often results in rapid regain and sometime even a weight gain that exceeds the starting weight.

Cellulite

Cellulite is not something children talk much about, but they may hear Mom address this issue. The truth is there is no such thing as cellulite. What companies that sell cellulite lotions and pads call cellulite is just fat deposits that bulge out between connective tissue, creating a ripply look. The only way these ripply bulges can be reduced is through a reduction in total body fat.

Water Pills

Diuretics are drugs that promote water excretion. These are not appropriate for children, and in adults they can produce water loss but not fat loss. Water weight loss will last only a day or so. Improper use of water pills or diuretics can lead to dehydration, a potentially serious condition requiring hospitalization.

Liquid Diets

Used for a limited time, as directed, or under a doctor's supervision, they can be effective for some people. They are not appropriate for children. It is very important that children learn, while they are young, that weight loss for them is based on calories in and calories out. During childhood their caloric needs are at their highest level, and a proper diet now is their best long-term chance at reaching their natural weight. For adults a liquid diet can sometimes give them a jump start on weight loss, but to be successful it must always be followed by a good diet and proper exercise. There is nothing magical about what is in the can either, it is just a fortified milkshake. It works for some adults only because the preportioned cans automatically limit calorie intake.

THE SEEDS OF AN EATING DISORDER ARE SOWN EARLY

A 1996 study in *Pediatrics* of over two thousand girls ages nine and ten found that 40 percent of these girls were already trying to lose weight, and that girls took up dieting behavior in response to their mothers' concern about their weight. In an earlier 1989 study almost half of the seven- to thirteen-year-olds surveyed were concerned about weight, and one-third had tried to lose weight, while 10 percent already exhibited characteristics that mimicked anorexia nervosa. These studies indicate that preadolescents are very interested in weight.

But don't go ballistic if your preadolescent or adolescent starts to experiment with a change in eating. A lot of young people turn to vegetarianism, count grams of fat, and even experiment with calorie counting or restriction. This does not mean your child has an eating disorder. In fact, food experimentation, particularly among young girls, is almost a right of passage or a bonding experience. This age presents a terrific opportunity to focus on health. If you have a preadolescent or adolescent interested in weight or fat, then seize the moment—don't leave her to diet magazines and unsound advice from friends. Go to the library and get a good medical book, check out the resources in chapter 9, or subscribe to a magazine that carries accurate health information such as *Prevention*. If your child is a vegetarian, then read the section about vegetarian eating that follows in this chapter or on page 271 in chapter 9.

If you feel your child's obsession with food or diets has gone beyond what is considered normal, then seek help. Eating disorders can include anorexia (starvation), bulimia (purging), or compulsive overeating. All of these eating disorders require professional intervention. You can start with your school nurse or family doctor or consult the resources listed at the back of this book, which provide information about eating disorders. Warning signs of an eating disorder may include the following behaviors:

Refuses favorite foods, obsessive scrutiny about food

Frequent trips to the bathroom

Unexplained disappearance of food

Distorted body image

Change in personality or behavior, mood swings

Denial that there is a problem

Hair loss

Stops eating with friends or family

Engages in vomiting

Uses laxatives, diet pills, or diuretics

Exercises compulsively

Complains of feeling cold

Poor sleep

Skin irritations

Chronic fatigue

Cessation of menstrual cycle

VEGETARIANISM

It is estimated that some twelve million Americans consider themselves to be vegetarian, and starting in late elementary school and early middle school young people
sometimes adopt this style of eating. Most parents, if they
are not vegetarian themselves, fear their children will
become nutritionally deficient on a meatless diet. Fortunately, nutrition deficiencies among vegetarians are not
commonplace. Only children and adolescents eating bizarre,
severely restricted menus are likely to be at risk. In truth
there is no one style of vegetarian eating but several levels.
(See What Kind of Vegetarian Are You? on page 29.) In
most cases when parents say their children are vegetarian
it means they eschew red meats such as beef, pork, and
lamb but still eat chicken and maybe even fish, often in the

form of tuna, and they drink milk. Such a diet does not meet the true definition of vegetarianism because it includes dairy and poultry, but you don't really need to make this point with children. Most young people choose a vegetarian diet for very admirable reasons such as the environment, ecological concerns, world hunger, or philosophical or ethical reasons. Ask your child about his or her reasons for eliminating meat. Children usually enjoy it when their family takes an interest in their changing eating habits. Don't let the vegetarian eater in the family rule the table, however, or make unpleasant remarks when family members choose to eat meat. Similarly, if the vegetarian child decides to sample a food that contains meat she should not be ridiculed or teased by siblings for doing so. Read more about planning a vegetarian diet in chapter 9, "Questions and Answers," page 271.

WHAT KIND OF VEGETARIAN ARE YOU?

Type	Foods Included
vegan	vegetables, fruits, grains, legumes, nuts, seeds
lactovegetarian	vegan diet plus milk, cheese, yogurt
lacto-ovo vegetarian	vegan diet plus milk products and eggs
fruitarian	fruits, nuts, olive oil, honey

IF RESTRICTIVE DIETS DON'T WORK, WHAT DOES?

Diets can be dangerous. In a growing child they could promote poor nutrition, but more important it could affect your relationship with your child and your child's self-esteem and her relationship to food. Many individuals I have counseled about food tell me they started restricted diets when they were young. This early dieting has made them feel guilty when they enjoy food and confused about what and how much to eat. A child whose parents restrict food when she is hungry will be forced to sneak and eat secretly. The child who does not lose weight as expected will feel that he has let his parents down, particularly if the parent has endorsed a restrictive plan. Parents are a young child's primary teachers, and your children will listen to what you say. Make sure you are telling them the truth about diets. The truth about diets is that 95 percent of people on restrictive diets regain the weight they lose, and when calories are too low the body can lose lean body tissue, and the body, fearing starvation, will lay down fat and become more efficient in weight retention, an effect that is the opposite of what the dieter hopes to achieve.

To help your child reach a weight that is natural, parents must create a food environment that is positive, one that provides access to the foods required to maintain health as well as the favorite foods your child enjoys. Parents need to create a pleasant, predictable, enjoyable feeding environment in the home. Parents must be accurately informed about their child's need for nutrition, and it is essential to find a place for regular exercise. Most of all it requires that good health be the family goal. The four areas that are important to your child to help him reach his natural weight are:

- effective parenting
- lifestyle and exercise
- accurate nutrition information
- family involvement

Making choices about food was one of the earliest health decisions you made when you started a family. And during the school years food is a powerful vehicle—meals can not only be pleasurable and provide nutrition but they can also allow a family to regroup together, and even make a child feel secure and confident. A landmark study of more than twelve thousand teenagers found that teenagers who grow up in families where they are given clear messages that they are cared about and that the parents are watching out for them engaged in a lower level of high-risk behavior that included drugs, alcohol, and early sexual activity. Food is an early and effective way to send a clear message that health requires personal responsibility and that you as a parent care and are paying attention. You picked up this book looking for advice on dealing with weight and you will find that information, but I believe a good diet can mean more than reaching a weight goal. Parents and families can use food and nutrition to send a message that their children's health is valued, and this has ramifications way beyond body size.

3

≡

Effective Parenting

Having a close relationship with one's children and spending time with them, for example by having dinner together on a regular basis, is strongly related to whether teenagers engage in risky behavior . . . such as drinking, fighting, or having sex at an early age.

—Teens and Their Parents in the Twenty-first Century: A government report by the Council of Economic Advisors

I don't know what to do. I know my son is overweight but I don't want to make him self-conscious. Please tell him the whole family needs a diet, not just him.

—Mother of a six-year-old boy

When I told the kids we were serving only fruits and vegetables for snacks they all groaned and rolled their eyes. But by Wednesday I couldn't slice and peel enough fruit to keep up with the demand. Parents should really know about this.

—Elementary school food service director during National Nutrition Month

Let your child know that you accept and love him, no matter what size he may be. Physical characteristics such as height and weight are not in a child's capacity to change, and parents have no control over their child's height and weight either. You can only control the quality of food purchased, the meal environment created, and the level of family activity. These are the areas where your focus should lie.

Your child absolutely needs your help to reach and maintain his natural weight, but that help cannot come in the form of control. Instead be a flexible, organized parent—a coach, not a dictator. Let these two principles guide you as you make decisions about food:

1. The principles behind feeding the overweight child are the same as for feeding any child.
2. How you parent is more important than the food you serve.

As in all areas of parenting we come to the job with preconceived ideas about how to do it. This chapter is going to ask you to examine your ideas, rules, and attitudes about food. It is possible that some of your assumptions and practices about food actually contribute to food struggles and negatively influence how your child eats and exercises. My advice to any parent concerned about his child's weight is to feed his child in the same manner that any child should be fed, regardless of weight—this means the emphasis is on health not weight loss. In chapter 7 you'll read nutrition advice about what to actually feed your child, but as I said earlier, how you parent is more important than what you feed your child. It will do no good if you prepare a beautiful, healthful meal and it goes uneaten because the child is too stressed or worried.

There are several areas that consistently emerge as trouble spots in the feeding relationship; they include guilt, misdirected responsibility, lack of trust, negative speaking, and parenting styles that are too controlling, too relaxed, use food inappropriately, or are misinformed about food and nutrition.

GUILT

If you are feeling guilty about your child's weight don't allow it to poison your relationship with your child or his relationship with food. Channel your worries into positive actions, but do not respond by imposing food restrictions. You cannot control what your child weighs; you can only control the things you can influence.

Your sphere of influence should cover the food that comes into the house, how the food is prepared and served, and how the family lifestyle evolves. I know you may want to put your child on a restrictive diet because there is an accepted (but unsubstantiated) belief that they work, but this is not true. Diets do not work and they actually do harm.

The truth is that your child is already on a diet. By definition the word *diet* means the customary and usual foods we consume. It is appropriate to examine your child's current diet to determine if it promotes health or not. Just as responsible parenting involves using seat belts and bike helmets, it also includes providing healthy food choices. It is your responsibility to have available the foods that will be best for your child. This may mean changing family food purchases, writing menus, using shopping lists, changing snack foods, and most important—setting a good example.

Kids tend to copy what they see siblings and parents do. For example, in Mexico children accept hot chili flavors because their older siblings eat them. In Japan children eat raw fish because they see their parents eat it. In the United States daughters diet because they see their mothers do it. Ask yourself: "What am I teaching my child by the way I eat and what I say?" "Is this the best I can do?" A parent's role is to offer a wide variety of good, wholesome food in a clean, orderly setting. It is the child's responsibility to eat it.

A parent's responsibilities include:

- Having wholesome food available
- Creating a pleasant eating environment (including a clean table, orderly meals, enforcing table rules about behavior)
- Creating opportunities for their child to be physically active
- Accepting their child's body size
- Protecting family mealtime by creating a time for the family to eat together on a regular basis

A child's responsibilities include:

- Having responsibility for food choices (choosing peas over carrots, a roll over bread)
- Determining when they are full or finished
- Adhering to family food rules—manners, trying new foods, etc.
- Participating at family mealtime in a manner appropriate for their age
- Being active and entertaining themselves

TRUST

Your child depends on you to feel secure about what and
how much he is eating; however you do not want to
become overinvolved in this area or you can create a
problem. It is ingrained in us as parents to think that we
are responsible for what our children eat, but in truth we
can't control what they eat, only what we offer. You must
trust your child to eat what he needs.

Left alone and given access to wholesome food a
healthy child will self-regulate food automatically. Over
sixty years ago researcher Clara Davis found that when
children were given nutritious choices they were able to
select a diet that was nutritionally adequate without adult
supervision. More recently Dr. Leann Birch studied fifteen children from two to five years of age by keeping
track of what they ate over a six-day period. What she
discovered was that children who ate little at one meal
compensated by eating more at the next meal, and at the
end of any given day they had consumed almost exactly
the same number of calories as the day before or the day
following. In other research Dr. Birch has found that
young children often refuse new unfamiliar food on the
first offering, but when the child is offered this item
repeatedly, five to ten times, it is eventually accepted.

In another article by Dr. Birch in the journal *Pediatrics*
she reports that 40 percent of parents surveyed believed
that restricting or forbidding a specific food would
decrease their child's preference for that food. Contrary
to what these parents believe research finds the opposite
to be true—restriction and prohibition actually enhance
the liking of the food and increase its consumption. A
parent who believes a food is bad in large amounts must

find a way to offer that food in small amounts so the child has the ability to self-regulate when older and more independent. Such can be the case with soda, ice cream, or chips. These are often identified by parents as "bad" foods, but prohibition at home won't help your child regulate these foods while at a friend's house or attending a school picnic. You have to help your child learn to self-regulate.

Parents often say to me, "If I let my child choose his own food he'll be eating nothing but macaroni and cheese and ice cream!" It is true kids will prefer those foods that are most familiar. I recommend that you have flexible family food goals (developed with good health as a goal). You will develop your own guidelines in chapter 7 but an example of a family meal goal might be that each meal contain a good protein source, a fruit, a vegetable, a starchy food, and a good source of calcium. In addition everyone is expected to try a taste of each food. This is called the One-Bite Rule (see page 39). This will require the macaroni and cheese eater to at least try the fruit and vegetable. If you keep offering a variety of foods and ask for his preferences his food repertoire will expand. Don't get excited if he is not a robust vegetable eater. Fruit carries almost the same nutrient profile, and when you read about nutrition in chapter 6 you will see that your child can get his nutrition from a wide variety of foods. You must make it safe for him to try new foods—he only has to taste it, not finish it. Trust your child; serve him wholesome food and he will eat what he needs. This approach is far better than forcing your child to eat. A healthy child will eat when hungry, and if a variety of wholesome, appealing foods are available that is what will be eaten. Remember: how you parent is more important than the food you serve. It may be helpful for you to think back on your own childhood experiences with food. Did your parents control food in a way that was positive? Do you want to practice the same parenting styles? For instance in my house I hated it when my mother would "sneak" food into stews or casseroles, yet I loved it when she let me help choose the vegetables served with dinner.

Some parents have said to me, "I ask him to try the carrots [or peas or whatever] but he refuses; he will never do it." My advice is to ask again but not to make a big deal about it at the dinner table. Do not force, do not cajole or get into a struggle; just ask. Later, when you child asks for your help—such as to find a toy, game, or bike—help with the task and use the opportunity to talk about what it means to listen to each other. Tell him that you listen to him when he makes a request and you help him when you can. Ask him to do the same with you. Ask him to try and do what you ask him to do when he can, and trying new foods is one of those things that is important. If you speak to your child with respect you will get the same in return. Remember that you cannot force your child to do anything (and if you do, you shouldn't). The only person you have control over is yourself. Your behavior and your relationship with your child are what will cause him to try new foods.

Part of the trust equation includes kids trusting parents to bring home or serve healthful foods. It is your responsibility as a parent to protect your children from a diet that is unhealthful. It is no longer possible for parents to be indifferent about the quality of their child's diet. Children today are drinking more soda than milk, more novelty snack foods than fruits and vegetables. The result is the obvious obesity epidemic, but less obvious is the rise in pediatric diabetes and the development of precursors to heart disease. There is very real concern that the incidence of osteoporosis, which causes brittle bones, will be epidemic in our children in adulthood because of their diet in childhood. It is our responsibility as parents to prevent this by protecting our kids from the food environment that may cause them illness. Protecting is different from controlling. For example, you teach a child to swim to protect him from drowning, but you don't refuse to let him near the water. With food, you protect him from a diet that is unhealthful by offering food choices that are the most nourishing, and you let your children know that eating wholesome food is something you value. There will be times when desirable but less nourishing foods are available and times when they are not. The secondary benefits of trust is that it makes for a strong relationship between parent and child.

THE ONE-BITE RULE

Young children like rules, and this one is easy and very effective. The purpose of the One-Bite Rule is to help your child feel safe about trying new foods, to widen her food repertoire, and to eliminate food struggles. It also creates an achievable goal and satisfies your responsibility to introduce your child to a variety of foods. Quite simply it means that all family members (this especially includes parents) must try at least one bite of every food served, even if it is a food they did not like in the past. If they try it and don't like it they can politely and discreetly remove it from their mouth, and if they like it they can have some more!

WATCH YOUR LANGUAGE

In our house, my daughters started talking about weight and being too fat at about age eight, even though my husband and I had been very careful not to criticize or praise ourselves or others because of weight or size. The message about weight simply filtered in through culture. I remember at age ten Emily saying to me, "Mommy, I want to lose weight." I said, "Fine. Cut off your hair and you'll lose about half a pound right away." "No, No," she said, giggling, "that isn't what I mean." "Well, then," I said, "say exactly what you mean." In an effort to uncouple the connection between weight and self-esteem I asked Emily what would be different if she weighed less. She said she wanted to feel strong and feel good about how she looked. "I want to lose weight" was not a goal that our family was going to support but feeling good about herself and feeling strong certainly were.

As a parent you want to set goals for your children that are positive. A goal of losing weight is a negative, it feels punitive. In our house we have family food goals that include: five fruits and vegetables daily, food purchases based on "real food," and the experience of eating should be pleasurable. In addition I have parenting goals for my children, which include teaching them how to cook, exposing them to a wide variety of food, supporting them to be physically active daily, and encouraging them to be media literate. These simple, well-defined goals promote health and end food squabbles. The goal of pleasure allows plenty of room for trips to the ice cream store and bakery, and since we have eaten our fruits and vegetables and maintain regular activity this presents no problem in regard to weight or health. It's just part of the joy of eating. When your child says, "I want to lose weight," start talking to him about developing a much bigger goal that includes food, health, and activity. He can be successful at this, and he will be much happier.

HOW TO TALK TO YOUR CHILD ABOUT WEIGHT

It can be awkward and difficult to talk to your child about his or her weight, but you can't ignore your child when he or she asks, "Do you think I'm fat?" Most children are not asking for the truth but for reassurance that they are okay and that you love them and they are acceptable. Respond by asking your child what she means and listen to the answer. If asked a difficult question such as "Should I start a diet?" and you aren't ready with an answer, then you can always be honest and say, "I can't answer that right now; let me think about it and we will talk later." Always, always remember to get back to your child. If you don't, then you may not be asked the next time and you have sent a message that there is something wrong with asking that type of question.

It would be best if you didn't wait for an issue to come up before you start talking about food and health. Become familiar with the Food Guide Pyramid and use it as a tool to guide the family toward healthy food choices. It is reproduced in chapter 6 along with an expanded list of foods to eat every day, sometimes, and occasionally. If your child says something like "I know you want us to eat differently because I'm too fat," switch the focus to health. Say something like "I want the whole family to eat differently because it is a healthy thing for us to do." This is a truthful and honest answer. Stress a positive message for your children that puts the emphasis on healthy eating and exercise, not dieting. This applies to both boys and girls, the regular-weight child as well as the over-weight child. Be an askable parent and let health be the goal that rules your decisions. Emphasize that everyone develops in his or her own way and everyone is unique.

One spring I attended a lecture for parents on eating disorders. It was a great session and its focus was on how parents can help their children not become preoccupied with dieting. But one parent raised a question that was hard to answer. She knew she did not want to start her ten-year-old on a "diet," yet both she and her daughter's physician were aware that her daughter was gaining weight at a rate that was unnatural for her height and age. So the question was, how do you address the problem without damaging a child's sense of self-worth? Here is where you fall back on principle number one: feeding the overweight child is the same as feeding any child, and all children must be fed a healthful diet. The question then becomes, what is a healthful diet for this child and is she getting it? Because she is gaining weight at an unnatural rate she is either not eating a diet that is healthy for her or she is not obtaining the level of activity she needs. It would be healthier for her to improve her diet or become more active. Again, move the focus from weight to health.

SPEAK POSITIVELY

Cultivate your family's identity as one that is concerned about food, nutrition, and health. You will do this when you develop family food goals in chapter 7 and communicate them to the family. Find something positive to say when speaking about your child and food. For example, a comment such as "Johnny is such a picky eater; he never takes more than one bite" is a negative comment that can be self-fulfilling, and if Johnny keeps hearing it he will never try more than one bite because that is what Mom and Dad says he does. A more positive comment might be: "Johnny is particular about what he eats, but what I like about him is that he always tries at least one bite of something new." This is more powerful, and because the way you speak affects behavior, positive comments are much more likely to promote healthful eating than negative ones. Let your child overhear you saying positive things to friends and other family members. You don't have to lie, simply find something positive such as "Julie loves her fruit but only when she gets to pick just the right one."

Do not let siblings label a child fat either. Disparaging remarks such as "piggy" or "chubby" are not funny and they are not harmless. Don't be sarcastic about your child's eating either. Be matter-of-fact and honest, never sarcastic. Even if the child laughs with you, sarcastic remarks are painful, and sarcasm can hurt your relationship and your child's sense of self-worth.

Never speak about your child as if they are not in the room. This is just plain rude. I have been in many situations where parents openly complain to me about their child's eating while the child stands by and cringes or worse yet beams at this negative attention. One of my golden rules about kids and food is to treat them and speak to them as if they were adults. For example, I would never serve an adult a food or beverage without first asking her if she wanted it. I would not make an adult eat all her salad or potato (or whatever) before she could have a slice of cake or another serving of the main entrée. Instead I am respectful and ask for her opinion, expecting her to know best what she prefers or when she is full. This same level of respect works perfectly with children too. Start with things like "Do you want milk or juice? Peas or carrots?" And if you are upset about a behavior such as not trying a new vegetable, tell the child directly that you are disappointed. "I would like you to try a taste of every vegetable. You don't have to eat it if you don't like it, just taste it." If you are unhappy that your child does not finish his milk or all the food on his plate, the next time allow him to serve himself less food and/or milk or go back for seconds. You can tell if you are speaking respectfully by asking yourself if you would say the same thing in the same tone to an adult. If the answer is yes, then you are speaking respectfully. When you speak respectfully to your child you have the right to demand the same behavior from her. If a child yells at you or is rude, explain to her that "I don't speak to you that way and I do not want you to speak to me that way." Some parents might think this gives too much adult-like power to a child. You are not turning control over to your child; instead you are setting an example of civility, acting as a good teacher—a coach, not a dictator.

PARENTING STYLE

How we parent will have a profound effect on every area of our child's life and this includes food. There is no perfect parenting style and none of us is the perfect parent, but there are some styles that can actually contribute to a child's overeating and for this reason they need to be examined. There are four styles of parenting that can contribute to a healthy child weighing more than his or her natural weight. These styles include a parent who is: too controlling, too relaxed, uses food inappropriately, or is misinformed about food and nutrition. The following quiz can help identify a parenting style that may interfere with or affect your child's weight.

Answer yes or no to the following questions:

1. Do you (or your spouse) allow your child to determine her portion sizes and avoid making her clean her plate?

2. Does your family have regularly scheduled mealtimes, eat in designated eating areas, and exercise regularly?

3. Do you (or your spouse) avoid using food as a bribe or punishment or as the exclusive reward for accomplishment?

4. Do you (or your spouse) know how much food your child needs to eat from each food group and how to evaluate the accuracy of nutrition and diet claims?

A no answer to any of these questions may identify an area of parenting that you should examine.

Question	Parenting Style
1.	Too controlling
2.	Too relaxed
3.	Food used inappropriately
4.	Misinformed about nutrition

TOO CONTROLLING

The controlling parent may do things such as predetermine her child's portions of each food served, insist that her child clean the plate, insist the child eat a certain number of carrots, apple slices, etc., or enforce rigid food rules such as no sugar in food or not more than one slice of bread per day or only four ounces of milk at a meal.

It can be very hard for a controlling parent to give up this role. Ellyn Satter, an expert on childhood feeding practices and family relationships, expressed it well when she wrote, "Overcontrolling parents may feel that letting go of control is the same as going out of control." The opposite is true; relinquishing control allows a child to regulate food intake accurately and flexibly. Strict parental control actually increases the preference for foods that the controlling parent is trying to control while limiting the acceptance of more varied foods. A parent that is too controlling actually interferes with and makes ineffective a child's response to his own natural, internal cues about hunger and fullness. A parent who strictly controls food intake will teach a child to doubt his ability of self-control. A child who is trusted to self-regulate learns self-esteem and personal responsibility. The controlling parent may create a food problem where one would not exist.

If you are caught in food struggles with your child, winning becomes bigger than the desired outcome. I once had a mother come see me because she was worried about her daughter's weight and eating. We talked at great length about her nutrition needs and how to set up a structure that worked for her family. Right before she left, while her daughter played in the waiting room, she broke down in tears and told me about the precipitating event that had brought her to see me. She had been at a family birthday party, a vegetable lasagna was served, and her daughter hated the chunky carrots and mushy broccoli it contained. In front of the extended family, my client told her daughter she had to eat the lasagna before she could have cake or participate in the party. Her daughter was unable to eat the lasagna and she sat at the table crying.

The mother felt awful, she never wanted this to happen, but once she made the rule and particularly with other family members looking on she felt she had to stick by what she had said. She came to see me because her worries about her child's nutrition were making her more and more controlling and her daughter was being more and more willful in resisting her control, which is exactly what any healthy human being would do. This is a classic struggle for the overcontrolling parent, and creating more rules will have the opposite effect of what you want to accomplish.

To get out of this controlling bind, establish family food goals and a plan of action that will work for you and your family (we'll do this in chapter 7); then you need to communicate these goals to your child in an age-appropriate manner. You need to be firm and consistent about these rules. Establish reasonable consequences when they don't work. For example, in the case of this party, if the One-Bite Rule had been in effect, the mother could have asked her daughter to try one bite. She would have, and that would have been the end of the issue. You also need to be flexible, and sometimes you should break your rules. For instance, when I'm in a situation where I am questioning how firm I should be about one of my food rules I ask myself whether this situation is going to be a recurring one or is it unique. The day after my niece's wedding my daughters asked if they could have leftover wedding cake for breakfast. Given that another wedding cake would not be available anytime soon, the girls had cake for breakfast and loved it. (Parties are often a time to relax food rules, but not rules about manners.) In another situation I had to stand firm. When my daughters started grade school and were away from home for both snack and lunch, they wanted "special" foods at both snack time and lunch. "Special" meant sweet, processed, bright-packaged stuff, not fruit, real juice, or homemade muffins. In this case I couldn't break our rules of five fruits and vegetables. Somewhere at lunch and snack they had to consume these or they just wouldn't get the nutrition they needed for growth. These rules are not meant as punishment. It would be easier to give in, but as a responsible parent, once you accept the important role food plays in your child's health you'll find it hard to be irresponsible. Your children will accept these rules too because they are communicated clearly and they are based on health not arbitrary whims. Once you've developed your family food goals, step back and relinquish the actual control of eating.

WON'T I SPOIL MY CHILD?

Parents worry that they will spoil their child if they give in to many food requests. You may spoil a child if you allow her to be the dictator. If you planned on serving fruit for dessert and your child demands ice cream and you give in because you fear your child will be mad at you if she doesn't get the ice cream, then your child is in charge and you are not parenting effectively. But allowing your child to choose her portion sizes or what type of vegetable or fruit she enjoys is a way of coaching your child toward independence. It will give her a message that you have confidence in your child's ability to make good decisions, and this is essential to her ability to self-regulate food.

TOO RELAXED

The too-relaxed parent may have no regular meal schedule or mealtimes, there may be unlimited access to calorie-rich food and drink, there may be no limit to screen time (TV and computer), there may be no promotion of physical activity. Though children are able to self-regulate food intake and make wholesome food choices, they must have access to wholesome food and have a predictable structure so they can self-regulate effectively.

In the absence of well-defined mealtimes and a designated place of eating, a child may "graze" throughout the day, eating an excessive number of calories because there is no clear, defined eating time. If the variety of food available in the home is heavily weighted on the quick and easy with a high sodium, sugar, or fat content a child may not be able to resist overeating because these foods do not contain fiber, protein, or water, nutrients that can signal hunger has been satisfied.

I remember meeting with parents of a three-year-old child who was significantly overweight. The child was given unlimited access to food considered healthy including puddings made with milk, flavored gelatin, low-fat yogurt, low-fat cookies. He ate these foods throughout the day and each night before bed. He was not served meals on a predictable schedule and was allowed to choose alternate foods whenever he was served a meal and did not like it. The result was that he trained himself to "graze" throughout the day. His desire for food was not due to hunger, it became an activity, and the absence of a well-defined eating schedule did not help him to self-regulate.

The feeding environment that is too relaxed allows for mindless eating. This is eating based on appetite not hunger, and it can account for hundreds if not thousands of calories in some families. The too-relaxed family may be able to improve their child's health simply by establishing a regular eating schedule, planning wholesome snacks, and limiting television.

Eating together as a family promotes a sense of togetherness. It socializes children, teaches them how to work within a group, how to use utensils, even how to share. I know after a busy day you may want to eat separately from your children, but your young children probably don't. Eating with your child will ensure better nutrition for the whole family, and food may even be better digested than when eaten in isolation. There are even academic benefits to eating family meals. Three- and four-year-old children who ate with their parents and were exposed to words at mealtime did better on picture vocabulary tests at age five than did children who did not have the same exposure to mealtime conversation.

If eating together seems impossible, look at the statistics, which show that most Americans try to fit it in. According to a 1990 *New York Times*/CBS poll 80 percent of families surveyed report eating together at dinner.

In the too-relaxed family, TV viewing may be an issue. A 1996 article in the *Archives of Pediatrics and Internal Medicine* examined the TV watching habits of 746 youths aged ten to fifteen and found that the odds of being over-weight were almost five times greater if the youths watched five hours of TV per day as compared to less than two. TV watching is linked with obesity for several reasons. TV watching does not burn calories and it takes time away from activities that do. Children eat mindlessly while watching TV, and TV advertising promotes high-calorie foods. If TV watching is unregulated in your family, consider a two-hour limit, or better yet, a no TV rule during the school week.

Most of us have similar goals for our children—we want them to be healthy, loving, socially caring, and successful in their schoolwork. Eating meals together on a regular basis is an effective and efficient way to meet all of these goals. The family meal is as important as soccer games, piano lessons, gymnastic classes, or other commitments that so often interfere with family time.

INAPPROPRIATE USE OF FOOD

The parent who uses food inappropriately may serve food to ease boredom, use food as the exclusive reward for accomplishment, or use food to elicit a preferred behavior such as being cooperative about chores. Excessive feeding may be seen as a way to cement a parent/child relationship. Food may be used as a reward or punishment by parents, or a child may use eating to ease or numb emotions such as anxiety, boredom, or anger.

If food is your exclusive response to rewarding good behavior or accomplishment, think of new ideas: take a walk with your child, read a book, buy him a favorite magazine or an inexpensive ball and play catch together, take him to the local pool, make a craft together.

If food is being used as punishment, just stop this type of punishment immediately. Feeding is one of the most important parental responsibilities you have. When you refuse your child the act of eating or participating at family mealtime you are excluding him from the family. You are breaking one of your responsibilities as a parent. It's similar to not allowing your child to go to bed when he is tired. Better to restrict TV, computers, or phone privileges as punishment but not food.

If your child is bored do not give food as a cure. I once counseled a mother of a four-year-old who was gaining significant amounts of weight. Her job required her to spend a lot of time in her car, and she brought her four-year-old son with her to save on day care. To keep him quiet and occupied while she drove or made quick stops she kept him busy with a supply of snack foods—granola bars, crackers, and fruit juice boxes. Every day he consumed many more calories than he used and steadily gained weight. When she switched to puzzles, book tapes, and games and used fruit as snacks, the weight was simply no longer an issue.

If your child is an emotional eater, meaning he eats out of boredom, stress, or anxiety, validate your child's feelings but come up with a solution other than food. Handle the emotion by asking what is wrong and listening carefully, but react with something other than food. Active play and exercise can be a healthy response to emotions such as boredom and even stress. Craft projects, writing, or any form of self-expression can be effective and a positive reaction to emotions.

The purpose of food is to be well nourished. The purpose of meals is to learn cooperation, to feel that you are part of a family, and to become well nourished. To use food as a reward, punishment, or to ease emotions is inappropriate, and it may contribute to a child's being overweight.

MISINFORMED

The misinformed parent may suggest their child try weight-loss drinks, diet supplements, or focus excessively on a specific nutrient. Parents often place great importance on specific foods or nutrients; milk and meat are foods parents often think their child needs more of than they actually do. Or a parent may allow unlimited access to "natural" foods because they are perceived as being more healthful.

Liquid calories are also a common source of misinformation. Liquid calories count as much as solid-food calories but are often not perceived to be a significant calorie source, yet they are. For example, are you aware that fruit juice carries the same number of calories as soda? Milk is a great calcium source, but it is also a liquid food, and a child does not need more than sixteen to twenty-four ounces in a day, even less if he's eating other calcium sources such as cheese, yogurt, or leafy green vegetables. If your child is on his second glass of milk at supper and he has already consumed several glasses earlier in the day you do want to switch from milk to water because he has already consumed enough milk to meet his need for calcium. Water is a calorie-free, appropriate beverage to quench thirst. (See Thirst Quenchers on page 137 for ideas on how to quench thirst.) Find out what foods and how much of each food your child really needs. You don't want to restrict your child's food intake, but you do want to give direction, and all children need direction. Advertisers know consumers like to see the terms "fat free," "sugar free," and "all natural" on labels. These terms sell more food, but they do not mean a food is healthier or that it can be consumed with impunity. You must help your child navigate what has become a complex food market. In general you can do this by becoming familiar with the nutrients foods should carry and keeping to the basics—lean toward simple, old-fashioned food, plain graham crackers not cream-filled cookies, whole fruit not fruitlike snacks. Do not restrict food intake at meals but find out what is appropriate for your child and let nutrition guide your decisions about what to serve at meals.

Parental Do's and Don'ts

Do's

Do respect your child.

Do teach your child about nutrition.

Do praise their efforts for eating well and exercising healthfully.

Do reassure them that they are okay no matter what size they are.

Do emphasize the importance of a good diet no matter what size an individual is.

Do teach your children not to tease anyone who is overweight.

Do use the phrase "What do you think?" frequently.

Do admit it when you do not know something.

Do admit it when you make a mistake.

Do listen to your child; show you are interested by asking questions.

Do watch television with your children. Talk about TV ads and how people look on television.

Do teach your children about how the body loses and gains weight.

Do be a role model for your children.

Do teach responsibility.

Do give clear direction.

Do let your children come up with solutions to problems.

Do foster independence; phase yourself out of the feeding equation.

Do insist that all family members speak to one another respectfully.

Do spend time together.

Do reinforce your child's competency beyond appearance.

Do give your child food chores—table setting, washing dishes, etc.

Do seek out local and ethnic foods.

Do teach your children to cook.

Don'ts

Don't speak to your child in a condescending manner.

Don't talk as if your child is not in the room.

Don't lecture about weight.

Don't blame yourself if your child's natural weight is greater than the norm.

Don't ignore your child's worries about his weight.

Don't be afraid to ask for help from counselors to manage disorganization or conflict.

Don't praise thinness; praise lifestyle.

Don't use phrases like "I look so fat" or "I need to go on a diet."

Don't eat exclusively at restaurant franchises.

To be an effective parent start with how you speak about food, health, and diets, and set family food goals. Become familiar with what your child needs nutritionally, decide on acceptable rules of behavior, discuss the need for exercise, and set a good example. In chapter 7 you will prioritize what you want to take on and where to start. Communicate your goals to your child.

I JUST CAN'T DO IT!

Change can feel unusual at first. If you find you are preoccupied with your child's weight and the suggestions I make here seem unnatural or impossible to carry out, you may want to speak privately with a family therapist. To help your child self-regulate you need to be a consistent but flexible parent. These are not easy traits to master if they are unfamiliar to you. While food struggles may seem like a trivial issue, one that your child will outgrow, and nowhere near the magnitude of the high-risk behavior we all might have to deal with when our children are older, the way a family deals with food issues when children are young is good practice for how a family will deal with more complex and dangerous conflicts when children are older. The groundwork of effective parenting laid in the early years around food and feeding issues will help your child achieve his natural weight and pay off in positive ways later on when your child is a teen and young adult.

4

≡

Exercise Is Essential

Over one-third of all parents (36 percent)
report their teens spend the majority of their
free time in front of a computer or television
screen.

—TALKING WITH TEENS: THE YMCA PARENT AND
   TEEN SURVEY

I hate it. Now that we are in junior high we
don't have a playground and when we do have
recess the boys hog the only basketball court so
we just sit around and do nothing.

—SEVENTH-GRADE STUDENT

If you found a program that would make your child
healthier, live longer, "feel good" about themselves, reduce
stress, raise self-esteem, and fight depression would you
encourage your child to use it? I'm sure your answer is
yes. The good news is that such a program is available to
you and your child right now and it costs nothing—it's
called regular exercise.

   The long-term health benefits of exercise, which
include lowering the risk for type 2 diabetes and lowering

blood cholesterol and blood pressure are not easily seen or measured in children, but the emotional and psychological benefits of exercise can be immediate. The next time your ten-, eleven-, or twelve-year-old comes home from school in a bad mood, feeling upset about a classmate's insensitive remark, or feeling they don't fit in, respond by taking them for a walk, a swim, a hike, or a bike ride—anything physical. The chemical changes that occur within our bodies when we move our muscles can actually relieve stress and boost our outlook on life. Try it and you be the judge of how effective exercise is to your child's emotional health.

There is plenty of research to support the role of exercise in improving physical health. Studies show that exercise improves the heart's ability to pump, and this prevents heart disease. It also reduces type 2 diabetes by increasing insulin sensitivity and improving carbohydrate metabolism. Regular activity protects against colon cancer and possibly other cancers such as breast cancer. Regular exercise helps build and maintain healthy bones, muscles, and joints. It also builds lean muscle tissue and reduces fat and helps control weight. To receive these health benefits physical activity must be continued into adulthood. It is believed that a child engaging in regular activity when young will continue this behavior into adulthood.

Unfortunately, according to the surgeon general's Report on Physical Activity and Health, about 14 percent of young people report no recent physical activity (about 25 percent of adults report no physical exercise during their leisure time). Girls are less active than boys, and black females are less active than white females. Only 19 percent of high school students are physically active for twenty minutes or more five days a week in physical education classes. As children get older and advance in school there is a striking decline in participation in physical activity. A 1997 survey by the National Association for Sports and Physical Education found that only one state, Illinois, mandates physical education from kindergarten through grade twelve. Many perceive physical education as "fluff," but it may actually help children learn more effectively. At a November 1999 conference in Boston, Massachusetts, entitled Learning and the Brain, researchers presented evidence that exercise improves blood flow and cell growth in humans, and research on mice found that learning actually improved with exercise. It is too soon to say that the active child will do better academically, but this positive connection between learning and activity is just one more reason to promote regular activity among our children. Of course, regular exercise is essential for your child to reach his natural weight. In one controlled study no weight loss occurred in a group of preadolescents participating in a diet program for sixteen weeks without exercise.

WHAT DO PARENTS AND KIDS SAY IT TAKES TO BE ACTIVE?

In the fall of 1996 a national, random phone survey of 1,504 households with children in grades four to twelve was conducted. The purpose of this interview was to assess current activity levels along with attitudes about exercise, willingness to be active, and what factors fostered activity. The survey was conducted by the nonprofit organization International Life Sciences Institute.

The phone survey found that children are not as active as they should be. Girls are less active than boys, yet they feel they are getting enough exercise. Parents say their children are not active because they lack the interest and would rather watch TV or play video or computer games. Children however say they aren't active because they lack time and have too much homework. According to parents in this survey, telling children that physical activity is good for them and encouraging activity makes no difference in activity levels. Yet, when children are asked, the children say parents can help through encouragement—playing with children, driving them to activities, watching their child in a sport, and telling them that exercise is good for their health. The survey also found that more students would use school facilities if supervised programs were made available. What this survey suggests is that with a little more support and promotion our young people would be more active.

How Much Exercise Do We Need?

There are no set exercise guidelines for very young children, and the truth is there really doesn't need to be. Give a young child the opportunity to be active by providing them with a safe place, active toys, and a little bit of encouragement, and voilà—they will be active. Elementary age children can meet their need for activity through active play, school playgrounds, school recess, school open gym, or a home swing set can provide a young child with the perfect opportunity to be active. But parents and the community must make these experiences available to young children.

The International Consensus Conference on Physical Activity Guidelines for Adolescents suggests that adolescents "be physically active daily, or nearly every day as part of play, games, sports, work, transportation, recreation, physical education, or planned exercise, in the context of family, school, and community activities" and that "all adolescents engage in three or more sessions per week of activities that last twenty minutes or more at a time and that require moderate to vigorous levels of exertion." In the Dietary Guidelines for Americans, released in the spring 2000 by the U.S. Government, children are asked to aim for sixty minutes of activity every day. Tag, jump rope, and active recess all count. In short, junior high and older kids should be active every day and work up a sweat, while being active, at least three times per week.

The adults in the family need to be active too because adolescents will start to take on the activity patterns of adults. Adults should be participating in some form of regular exercise three to five times a week. The Dietary Guidelines for Americans suggest thirty minutes of activity most days of the week. Adults, but not adolescents, need to include a strength training workout two to three times per week—this means working with weights or machines that build muscle mass. If you're looking for a way to spend quality time as a family or with your child, consider starting a walking, hiking, or biking program.

BE FLEXIBLE

Teach your children to stretch as part of their overall fitness goals. A program of proper breathing and stretching will prevent injuries and aid relaxation. You can also try making a game out of it by seeing who can touch their toes—girls are often more flexible than boys. For guidance on effective stretching get your hands on a copy of the book *Stretching* by Bob Anderson. See references for chapter 4.

WHAT TYPE OF EXERCISE?

Exercise can be anything that works up a sweat. For young children try putting on their favorite Disney sound track and let them dance or encourage active play like capture the flag, tag, or hopscotch.

Vigorous swinging or playing on a hammock or a climbing gym are all great activities. Before age ten, children spontaneously engage in physical play when given the opportunity. But older children can be less active and actually need to be encouraged to find a regular activity they can call their own.

Organized sports can be a good form of exercise for many capable children. Sports that require a team, however, won't provide much exercise when there is no team to play with or if your child spends a lot of time on the bench. Of course, if your child will practice soccer drills or shooting hoops or other sport skills on his own, this can be good exercise. Unfortunately, at around age thirteen kids start to drop out of organized sports, perhaps because there is more competition to obtain a place on a team. Young children can get turned off by an activity if they experience failure at an early age. I find that by the time junior high rolls around if a child does not see himself as athletic he or she no longer pursues organized sports. And an overweight child may feel even less capable than a normal weight child.

In my opinion organized sports are only one part of the exercise puzzle for our kids. Each child needs to find an activity that suits him or her. After age twelve a regular walking or running program can be a great form of exercise. I like it because it does not need to be competitive unless you join a team. Parents should encourage and practice lifestyle exercise that increases energy expenditure in regular activities. Examples include taking the stairs, walking when possible instead of driving, and using some form of activity to relax instead of television.

How to Help Kids Be More Active

Safety can be a real issue for kids. For today's children obtaining the exercise they need can be complicated—don't blame them. We need better wellness and fitness programs for our kids and families. Schools should be encouraged to offer open gym time before school starts. Physical education should be provided in school, and enjoyable exercise opportunities must be made available to all kids. Remember that children are motivated 100 percent by fun. That is why games like tag and kickball may be more successful than running around a track a specified number of times. Many fast-food restaurants are adding indoor gyms in the form of "playhouses" for their young customers. This is a wonderful addition. Anyone who has seen a child scurry through these tubular mazes and reappear sweating and red-faced knows their kid has gotten a good dose of exercise.

Friends and family members who encourage and set an example will have a positive effect on children. If Mom and Dad or a favorite aunt, uncle, or even neighbor are active they can be a powerful role model. You can support your child by giving birthday gifts of running shoes, skates, or a soccer ball or basketball. It is also important that your child's health care provider encourage your child to be physically active. The goal behind being active is to be healthy and strong. The secondary benefits may include weight loss, but because of the health benefits of exercise all family members are encouraged to be active no matter what size they are.

YOU CAN BE HONEST

I often tell clients there are two types of people in the world: those who love to exercise and the rest of us, who have to make ourselves do it. If being active does not come naturally to you, you don't have to pretend it does. You can tell your child you are not going to watch TV or read the paper but take a walk instead, because you know it is important to your health. This sets a wonderful example for your child. You can even ask your child to help you reach your exercise goals and at the same time help your child reach hers.

HOW TO GET YOUR CHILD TO BE MORE ACTIVE

An increase in activity won't happen just by talking about it. Start by talking to your child, but then come up with a realistic plan of action. Let your child know that regular exercise is important to the family, and just as you want her to find time to read, do chores, and do homework, it's just as important to find time for exercise. Always remember young children are motivated by fun, so get their input on what they want to do. If your child is overweight he may feel uncomfortable in organized sports—solo activities such as biking, walking, or swimming can be better choices.

The entire family being active on a regular basis will set an example for the children. Parents can help by deliberately parking farther away from the store and taking the stairs instead of the elevator. A 1995 study of preschool kids found that children with overweight parents had lower levels of physical activity and ate a diet higher in fat and lower in carbohydrate. Such research clearly indicates the effect parents have on their child's health. Parents need to teach moderation in activity too. The idea of "no pain, no gain" is not true for children. Don't compete with your child either; competition with Mom and Dad or even other siblings may decrease enthusiasm and participation. Remember, the purpose of being active is to be healthy, not to win—downplay competition.

If your child is interested, consider organized sports. Schools usually have a variety of teams. Talk to the school physical education teacher to find out what's available and what would be appropriate for your child. Find out who is coaching the team and what their philosophy is. Before senior high school the focus of team sports should be on building team spirit, learning fundamentals, and obtaining exercise. Winning can come later. Other sources of organized activities include your town recreation department, YMCA and YWCA clubs, Boy Scout and Girl Scout clubs. Call a neighboring town to see what their recreation departments offer, usually the bigger the community the wider the offerings. You can also seek out private lessons for dance class, karate, gymnastics, tennis, or find a public pool where your child can take lessons or join a swim team. Lots of children will enjoy a team or class better if they have a buddy or someone else they know in the class.

Exercise Do's and Don'ts

Do's

Do be a role model for your child. If you are active, your child is more likely to be active.

Do talk to your child about the importance of exercise.

Do admit if you find it difficult to be as active as you should (this is true for most adults).

Do plan family activities that involve exercise. Take a walking tour of a city. Go for a hike, rent a canoe, go swimming or biking.

Do be sensitive if your child is overweight. She may tire easier or feel less comfortable among active youngsters.

Do reduce the amount of sedentary activities your child engages in such as computer games, TV watching, and so on.

Do use stairs and walk to school or a friend's house when possible.

Do encourage nonperformance sports such as walking, hiking, recreational swimming.

Do plan for activity. Make a plan to take a walk on weekends or before dinner.

Do make sure activities are safe.

Do make it fun.

Do provide a variety of experiences.

Do keep active toys around—balls, bats, roller skates, jump rope, hula hoop, Frisbee, paddleball, bicycle, badminton, volleyball, tetherball, Ping Pong, hop-scotch, four square.

Do ask your child about fitness goals.

Do encourage your school board to promote and provide for physical activity.

Do volunteer to coach or assist in team sports.

Do teach safety rules.

Do ensure coaches have team goals that match the age of the players.

Don'ts

Don't compete with your child.

Don't become obsessed with activity. Remember, exercise is meant to promote health; overdoing it can lead to injury.

Don't compare your child's athletic ability to others'.

Don't support the "no pain, no gain" philosophy of exercise.

Don't use physical exercise as punishment.

Regular exercise will prevent a myriad of ailments when your child is older, and it will increase your child's energy expenditure. The more immediate gains for your child can include a more optimistic outlook on life and an improved sense of strength and competence. Your child does not have to be a champion athlete to receive these benefits; all that is required is a commitment to increased activity, and it can be in any form that suits your child. The success will come when your child fulfills the goal he or she sets. Quite simply, people and children feel their best when they do what they set out to do. In the case of exercise the goal does not need to be winning, and it should not be for the sole purpose of losing weight. The reason you want to encourage exercise is for the sake of being healthy and as strong as possible. Set achievable activity goals with your child and family and judge the benefits for yourself.

5

≡

Your Child Needs
Real Food

How is it that we Americans, perhaps the most
health-conscious of any people in the history of
the world, and certainly the richest, have come to
preside over the deadly fattening of our youth?

—GREG CRITSER, *HARPER'S MAGAZINE*

Obesity continues to increase rapidly in the
United States . . . strategies and programs for
weight . . . must become a higher public health
priority.

—A. H. MOKDAD, *JOURNAL OF THE AMERICAN MEDICAL
ASSOCIATION*

The federal government's largest nutrition-
education program for the general public—
the "5 a Day" program—has a pathetic
communications budget of $1 million.
Meanwhile, companies like Coca-Cola and
McDonald's spend over $11 billion per year on
advertising.

—CENTER FOR SCIENCE IN THE PUBLIC INTEREST YEAR
2000 REPORT

You will not help your child reach her natural weight by depriving her of food or by controlling what she eats. In order to be successful at reaching and maintaining natural weight you must turn control of food over to your child and trust her body to do its own self-regulating. However, you must stack the cards in her favor by providing access to food that I call real. Real food is food that is minimally processed and continues to carry most of the nutrients it was grown with. Real fruit carries vitamin C, real vegetables contain vitamin A, and real grains still have measurable amounts of fiber. These foods are good sources of the naturally occurring phytochemicals that fight disease, and they are your best hope for helping your child reach and maintain her natural weight because they can help control appetite naturally. Real food may have fat removed, such as trimmed meats or low-fat dairy products, but it will not be artificially manipulated to be fat free and it is naturally low in salt and sugar.

There is now enough research completed to definitively say that our food choices will determine our health and weight. Much of this research has been done with adult subjects, and some of the best studies come out of the Harvard University's Nurses Health Study and the Health Professional Study. The health benefits for adults of eating real food can apply to our young people too. In fact, the research on adults supports the commonsense notion that what we feed our children will have a lifetime effect on their health. If you fill your child's plate with real food, she will eat only what she needs, and she'll have important secondary benefits including less illness, an improved sense of well-being, and an appreciation of food that will last a lifetime.

WHAT IS DIFFERENT ABOUT OUR FOOD AND FOOD SUPPLY TODAY?

There has been a dramatic change in our food supply during the twentieth century, and it continues into the twenty-first century. In the 1930s our ancestors would have had approximately nine hundred food items to choose from in the food market. Today an American supermarket can carry forty thousand food items, and one thousand new items are added each month. These new foods have been developed to make life easier for us— many are convenience, ready-to-eat, and frozen foods. The availability of frozen vegetables, fruits, frozen juice, even frozen meats is a real time and money saver, and it can add to the nutritional quality of our menu. There are also many more ethnic foods and imported produce available to us today. When I was a kid I never heard of a kiwi fruit or a mango, yet today these are my children's favorite fruits.

But among the real food is an enormous amount of highly processed, refined foods. Refined foods provide calories and carry some nutrition, but they are made inexpensively and are heavily processed. Enhanced with sodium or sweetners to add flavor, advertised heavily, and packaged attractively they are consumed by children in excess. Such food will either be missing the nutrients contained in a real food or they will have excessive amounts of sodium or sugar. When a food carries the flavor but not the nutrients found in the real thing, such as fiber, and a natural balance of sodium and sugar, children are apt to overeat that food. For example, one serving of real fruit should contain about 70 calories, 15 grams (g) of total carbohydrate, 1 to 2 g of fiber, 35 milligrams (mg) vitamin C, little or no sodium, and traces of many more hard-to-measure but very important nutrients and phytochemicals, and it carries appetite-controlling moisture. An apple, banana, orange, even watermelon all fit this nutrition profile easily. Processed, refined fruitlike products carry more calories, more sodium, and less of the essential nutrition our children need. A fruit snack bar carries 80 calories, 16 mg vitamin C, 18 mg sodium, and less than 1 g of fiber; a 50-calorie fruit roll contains 10 mg vitamin C, no fiber, and 54 mg of sodium. These refined foods are often marketed to replace traditional, real food (such as fruit drink over fruit juice, and so on). It is occasionally okay to eat a refined food, but many of the food items stocked on supermarket shelves, particularly as snack items, fit the description of highly processed, refined food much better than they do that of real food, and we are eating them in excess and gaining weight.

In addition to a wide variety of new foods, there is an abundant supply as well. It is estimated that the average adult male needs about 2,500 calories daily and females approximately 2,000 calories. A very broad guideline for children is 1,000 calories plus one hundred calories for each year of age. That means an eight-year-old needs 1,800 calories every day, a ten-year-old 2,000. The current American food industry produces enough food to provide each American with 3,800 calories every day. Human beings have survived periods of food scarcity because we have the ability to store unneeded calories as body fat. Unfortunately because food is now so plentiful, this eat-and-store formula now works against us.

HOW REFINED FOOD MAY CAUSE
YOUR CHILD TO OVEREAT

Remember that hunger is controlled by the hypothalamus in the brain. Changes in blood sugar, fatty acids, insulin levels, and electrolytes in the blood send messages to the hypothalamus that the body is hungry. This is physical. The same system can send messages of satiety or fullness. A menu that carries a lot of liquid calories or refined carbohydrates may override this system because they do not signal the satiety message. Because we are biologically programmed to desire and enjoy the taste of salt and sugar, food enhanced with these tastes may increase our appetite, causing us to overeat. Satiety is signaled by a full stomach, and foods that carry a high moisture and fiber content will signal satiety. Foods low in moisture and fiber and high in fat, salt, or sugar will keep us eating, even when not hungry. For this reason human beings are less likely to eat a whole bag of apples than they are a bag of chips.

Appetite is a learned psychological response to food. Advertising and the wide availability of refined, salty, sweet foods can quite easily cause a child to have an appetite even when not hungry. Not only will real food help your child attain and maintain his natural weight, but it will also help her resist disease in old age, perhaps even middle age. It will probably help her concentrate in school better, and may reduce the number of colds and flu she has each year. The health benefits contained in real food are the reason a thin child as well as an overweight child needs to eat real food. Kids often say to me, "My little brother gets to eat and drink anything because he's skinny." I cringe when I hear this because in this case it sounds like the little brother is eating foods that replace real food, and this can mean the child is not getting the health-promoting benefits of real food. In a study of one thousand families it was found that only about one of the three to five recommended servings of fruits and vegetables were being eaten daily, and only 12 percent of the families in the survey were eating the minimum six servings per day. However, consumption of sweets and fats is strong. Americans indulge in sweet, fatty foods about eight hundred times per year, more than twice a day. Remember the *Pediatrics* study mentioned earlier; of the three thousand young people surveyed, all were eating below the recommendations for every important food group accept the dairy or calcium group.

There is a place for fun and special food in every child's menu, it just can't be at the expense of the real food your child needs. Otherwise it can lead to an unnatural weight gain and poor health when older.

FIBER, HEALTH, AND WEIGHT CONTROL

Real food quite simply prevents disease. In 1996, Dr. E. B. Rimm of the Harvard School of Public Health published the results of a study begun in 1986 that followed 43,757 U.S. male health professionals. The purpose of the study was to discover the health benefits of fiber and its effect on the risk of coronary heart disease. The participants, forty to seventy-five years of age, were free from heart disease when they entered the study, and they each completed a detailed diet questionnaire. During the six years of follow-up 734 of the men experienced a heart attack. Dr. Rimm found, as he reviewed food questionnaires and the heart health of the participants, that as fiber intake increased the risk of heart attack went down. Specifically it was the fiber from cereals and grain foods that lowered the risk, not the fiber from fruits and vegetables. The study revealed that for each increase in cereal fiber of 10 grams, the risk of heart attack dropped by 29 percent. This means that cereal-based food such as fiber-rich cereals, whole wheat bread, whole grain cereal, whole grain muffins, and brown rice all have a heart protecting effect and should be part of a healthy diet daily for adults and children. Why cereal fiber has this protective effect is not entirely understood. It may be the fiber but it may be that these less-refined foods carry magnesium and vitamin E, which offer protective effects.

Like the Health Professionals Follow-up Study for Male Health Professionals, another Harvard School of Public Health study known as the Nurses Health Study, the largest long-term study of women in the world, examined the dietary habits of over sixty-five thousand nurses, found that eating more high-fiber foods can prevent type 2 diabetes, the form of diabetes linked to weight gain and age but also on the rise in children. The highest risk of this type of diabetes was found in women who consumed low amounts of cereal fiber and drank sweetened cola beverages and white bread. It is believed that refined or processed food is linked with type 2 diabetes because the carbohydrate in such food is rapidly absorbed into the bloodstream, causing the pancreas to put out more insulin in an attempt to keep blood sugar within normal limits. Switching from white bread to whole wheat bread, white rice to brown rice, sugary breakfast cereal to whole grain cereal, and presweetened yogurt to plain yogurt mixed with fruit may give your child the same diabetes protection the nurses on the high fiber diet had, and it can be accomplished deliciously.

More recently in a 1999 issue of the *Journal of the American Medical Association* it was reported that women who consumed more fiber from cereals and grains, about 8 grams daily, had a 37 percent lower risk of heart disease compared to women who consumed about a third as much. In addition to the protective effect cereal grains have on the heart, epidemiological studies find a strong protective effect against cancer, specifically gastric and colon cancer.

In another study, this time on young adults ages eighteen to thirty participating in the Coronary Artery Risk Development in Young Adults (CARDIA) program, the participants' fiber consumption predicted their insulin levels, weight gain, and coronary vascular disease factors more accurately than their total fat or saturated fat consumption. This suggests that fiber may protect against obesity by lowering insulin levels. This study supports an earlier *Pediatrics* article by Dr. S. Y. Kimm. He discovered that obesity is rare in developing countries where fiber intake is high, probably because the fiber reduces the caloric density of food, slows digestion, and affects satiety. The author suggests that increasing fiber in a child's diet may help promote satiety at meals and curb hunger between meals.

Another reason to encourage your child to eat more fiber and unrefined grains is for the nutrition they carry. Dr. Hambidge studied the zinc status of healthy children living in Denver and found that marginal zinc status may be a problem in American children. Rapid growth requires zinc, and zinc-rich foods include poultry, lean meats, low-fat and nonfat dairy, legumes, and particularly whole grain products.

Children between two and twelve need 7 to 17 grams of fiber respectively each day, and adults need at least 25 grams. Yet most children do not meet this recommendation because they eat a menu heavy in refined cereal and bread. As a result they are missing the protective effects of cereal fiber demonstrated in these studies.

The protective effect of whole grains—wheat, rice, corn, oats, rye, barley, triticale, sorghum, and millet—goes beyond their fiber content. Clearly they carry protective substances that help us resist disease and control weight. Yet unless you are making a concerted effort to put whole grains onto your child's plate I can almost guarantee that your child is not getting the protection he needs. Start looking at the fiber content on the nutrition facts panel. Every grain-based food such as cereal, bread, and many snack foods should contain fiber.

GRANDMA WAS RIGHT—EAT YOUR VEGETABLES!

The Nurses Health Study has also reported that generous amounts of certain vegetables can reduce the risk of heart attacks, stroke, and early death in women. There is a tremendous amount of data that supports the link between a high intake of fruits and vegetables and a reduced risk for disease. Fruits and vegetables are a rich source of vitamins, minerals, fiber, and a wide range of phytochemicals. These phytochemicals seem to have many influences on our health. They stimulate the immune system, reduce platelet aggregation, help control cholesterol, reduce blood pressure, and even provide an antiviral effect. There is also a causal link between vegetable and fruit consumption and activity. In epidemiological studies, the frequency of fruit and vegetable intake goes up as an individual's level of activity increases. People who eat few fruits and vegetables report less activity, more heavy drinking and heavy smoking. I like to think that people who exercise like to eat well and that people who like to eat well like to exercise. Whatever the connection is, it's a good one, and maybe if we get our kids eating well they'll exercise more, or exercise more and want to eat better.

There are specific fruits and vegetables that are standouts for their health benefits. Tomatoes show promise in their ability to protect against cancer, specifically stomach, colon, and bladder cancers. It is speculated that lycopene, a naturally occurring phytochemical abundant in tomatoes, is responsible for this protection. Blueberries, strawberries, raspberries, and blackberries all contain anthocyanin, a chemical that gives fruit its reddish-blue color and protects against lung, skin, and espophageal cancer. Carrots, apricots, papaya, sweet potatoes, mangos, and fruit are all rich sources of beta-carotene, a potential cancer-fighting chemical. Red grapes contain a chemical known as resveratrol, which is credited with battling different forms of cancer. Dark green leafy vegetables rich in folic acid, a B vitamin, protect against heart disease, and one of the reasons why the Japanese and Chinese have lower rates of breast and prostrate cancer may be their high soy intake.

There is a mountain of information that links the ingestion of fruits, vegetables, and unrefined grains to lowering the risk of serious disease. So great is the link between diet and cancer that in 1997 the Center for Cancer Prevention at the Harvard School of Public Health concluded that cancer is a preventable disease. Researchers estimate that two-thirds of all cancer deaths can be linked to smoking, diet, obesity, and lack of exercise.

All the major health organizations, from the American Heart Association to the American Dietetic Association to those affiliated with the U.S. government, recommend that Americans young and old, thin or fat, eat a minimum of five fruits and vegetables (and more would even be better) and at least six servings of grain foods daily (half of these as whole grain).

THE WEIGHT CONTROL BENEFITS OF REAL FOOD

In 1999 the Centers for Disease Control and Prevention released an alarming observation about children's food and weight. In 1997, in low-income households, almost 9 percent of two- to four-year-old children were overweight. This is up from 7 percent in 1989. An almost 2 percent climb in one decade is disconcerting, particularly in this age group. When a young child gains weight from empty-calorie food, not only does the increase in body fat adversely affect health, but such a diet will also not provide the health benefits that could protect against the effect of excess weight. These kids are obtaining an unnatural weight probably because of the food they select.

This effect is probably not limited to young, poor children. In March of 1999 David S. Ludwig, M.D., the director of the Obesity Program at Children's Hospital in Boston, published a study in the journal *Pediatrics*. Dr. Ludwig's study found starchy, sugary foods contribute to a child's overeating. The researchers looked at the effect foods with a high dietary glycemic index (GI) had on intake. Glycemic index is a measure of the effect food has on blood-sugar level after eaten. Foods with a high glycemic index are rapidly digested and absorbed, and changed into blood sugar or glucose. Food with a high glycemic index can include breads, cereals, pasta, and table sugar. Low glycemic index foods include vegetables, beans, and fruit.

In this study twelve obese teenage boys were evaluated on three separate occasions. In each session they were asked to eat a meal at breakfast and lunch that had either a low, medium, or high GI. All meals had an equal caloric value, and they were allowed to eat as much as they wanted after lunch, at which time the researchers kept track of how much they ate. They found that after the high-GI meal the boys were hungrier and ate more. Their food intake was 53 percent greater than after the medium-GI meal, and 81 percent greater than after the low-GI meal. The researchers concluded that the rapid absorption of glucose after eating the high-GI meals caused a series of hormonal and metabolic changes that promoted overeating in these obese boys. The boys also reported greater hunger after eating the high-GI meal than the low-GI meal. This is only one study, but it strongly suggests that eating a diet that is high in refined grain products can set in motion a series of internal events that can cause a child to overeat and feel more hungry. Conversely a diet high in fruits, vegetables, and legumes, all foods with a low GI, may help reduce hunger and overeating.

LIQUID CALORIES COUNT TOO

Richard Mattes, a researcher at Purdue University in Indiana, reviewed more than forty food studies and found that people do not compensate liquid calories as they do solid food calories. Dr. Mattes's remarks were cited in an

April 1999 issue of *The Nutrition Action Healthletter.* The research suggests that when we eat solid food we automatically compensate by eating a bit less, but when soda, juice, or clear liquids are consumed, such compensation in calorie intake does not occur.

One USDA survey finds soda consumption is soaring. In 1970, Americans consumed approximately twenty-five gallons per year per person. In 1980 it moved to thirty-five gallons, and in 1995 soda consumption was up to fifty-three gallons per person per year. If it is true that liquid calories are not as effectively compensated for as solid food calories, the increase in soda consumption may explain at least in part the rise in our rate of obesity. Fruit juice is probably not without its problems either. In January 1997 the journal *Pediatrics* published an article entitled "Excess Fruit Juice Consumption by Preschool-Aged Children Is Associated with Short Stature and Obesity." The researchers recruited ninety-four two-year-old children, and seventy-four five-year-old children. Each child completed a seven-day diet record. Nineteen of the children drank more than 12 ounces of fruit juice per day, 42 percent of these children had short stature versus only 14 percent of the children who drank fewer than 12 ounces per day. Obesity was more common among the children drinking 12 ounces of juice per day. After adjusting for maternal height, child age, and gender, the children who drank more than 12 ounces per day of fruit juice were shorter and more overweight. The researchers conclude that limiting fruit juice to 12 ounces per day can be beneficial to a child's health. However, researchers from the University of Texas and the Gerber Products Company refute this claim. They interviewed 105 children two to three years of age and had registered dietitians complete twenty-four-hour recalls with the children and two-day food records. They concluded that there was no difference in height or BMI and that their research does not support the earlier researchers' recommended limit of 12 ounces of fruit juice per day for children.

However, if you are concerned about your child's weight and health it is prudent to look at her liquid calories as well as solid food consumption. Since liquids can add calories without curbing appetite you want to help your child limit her intake. Today's beverages are often packaged in child-friendly sizes and in pretty packaging. And just because the packaging claims it is natural or contains fruit juice does not actually mean it will promote good health. Think about why you serve a beverage. If it is for nutrition, then serve a nutritious real-fruit juice. (I recommend orange, grapefruit, pineapple, and vitamin C–fortified apple juice). If it is to quench thirst, then offer water or water flavored with a small amount of juice. Read about recommended thirst quenchers on page 137. Using fruit juice blends and sports drinks to quench thirst can add a lot of extra, unneeded calories, which kids may not be able to compensate for. In addition, many of these fruit drinks are loaded with extra sugar (usually in the form of high-fructose corn syrup) and have a high GI, which may make your child even hungrier and cause more overeating.

SUGAR: THE FASTEST GROWING FOOD GROUP

The average American eats twenty teaspoons of sugar per day. That's about 80 grams. The Center for Science in the Public Interest recently began a campaign requesting that the Food and Drug Administration set a maximum Recommended Daily Value for sugar of 40 grams per day, or ten teaspoons of added sugar per day. Sugar is not inherently bad, it is simply a carbohydrate that is changed into glucose in the blood and provides energy. The problem with sugar is that it is so appealing it is hard for humans, particularly kids, to resist its allure. Remember, we are biologically programmed to eat sweet food: food that tastes sweet is not likely to be poisonous, and that is probably why, from an early age, children prefer sweet tastes. Food companies recognize this preference and have laden their products with added sugar (usually in the form of HFCS, read about HFCS below) to entice our kids to eat more. For example, unsweetened spoon-size shredded wheat biscuits carry 1.3 percent sugar per serving, frosted mini wheats carry 33.6 percent sugar. Which product do you think your child will be most likely to overeat? Which one costs more? The sweetened one. In this case the presence of sugar is obvious. Less obvious is its inclusion and abundance in snack items and food you would not expect to carry much sugar, such as peanut butter, granola bars, all natural juices and natural fruit snacks. The addition of sugar can cause overeating, and its presence is more prevalent than you think. Another danger of sugar-laden foods is that they can crowd out more nutritious foods. Today, teenagers drink as much soda as milk, but in the 1970s teenagers consumed twice as much milk as soda. The problem with this change is that 92 percent of bone mass is accumulated by age eighteen, thus it is in these teen years that calcium is so important. If milk is being replaced by soda it will lead to unhealthy bones when older. Why do you think there is more soda being consumed today? Because it is heavily advertised and very profitable.

Food companies don't use the same form of sugar you use in your kitchen. They use high-fructose corn syrup

(HFCS) and combine HFCS with other sweeteners such as sucrose, dextrose, and maltose to make even more appealing sweet tastes. HFCS is corn syrup that has been treated with enzymes to make it taste sweeter. The result is a very sweet, inexpensive additive that is found extensively in sodas and snacks. HFCS and sugar blends are so prevalent that they are permanently affecting our children's perception of what they consider sweet. For example, buy a ready-made muffin or prepare muffins from a mix that uses HFCS and compare it to a homemade batch that uses old-fashioned cane sugar. Ask your kids which they prefer. Chances are they will prefer the muffins from the mix because of its sweeter taste. This indoctrination to very sweet-tasting food may increase their taste threshold for sweets and may cause overeating.

There is absolutely a place for sweet-tasting food in your child's diet. It's called dessert. The problem today is the abundance of sugar-rich food that is served at mealtime and at snack time too. Eating a high-sugar diet puts your child at risk of not being able to self-regulate his food and drink intake. For fun, peruse your cupboard and read labels. Look at your child's favorite foods. If HFCS is on the label it may be causing a problem of overeating. The solution is to get back to real foods, which don't have a heavy dose of added sugar in the form of HFCS. Use food labels to compare the sugar value in similar products. You can enroll your child in this project too. Remember you are the coach, not the dictator; with age they can start to read labels and understand the food goals your family hopes to achieve. As a parent it is simply your job to establish family food goals and communicate them to your child. It is essential that you establish family food goals and basic meal do's and don'ts. If you don't set these goals the food companies will, and their message is—eat our food and lots of it!

SUGAR AND FOOD LABELS

Sugar is listed on the nutrition facts panel under carbohydrate. Each 5 grams of sugar theoretically is equal to one teaspoon of sugar. The sugar content listed on the label lumps together all types of sugar. Some foods such as milk, yogurt, even cheese and dried fruit look as if they carry a large dose of sugar, but dairy foods, fruits, vegetables, and even some foods in the grain/starch group naturally carry sugar as an integral part of the food. For this reason the sugar content on labels is most useful when comparing different brands of the same food product, such as a Triscuit cracker to a Ritz cracker or Jiff peanut butter to Teddy's peanut butter, or Tropicana orange juice to the Minute Maid brand.

SALT, JUST AS TASTY AS SUGAR

Do you remember the slogan for a popular potato chip that threatened, "I bet you can't eat just one"? That slogan could actually be applied to any chip, and most snack foods as well. Much like sugar, human beings enjoy the taste of salt, and when it is in combination with fat it is almost irresistible—hence the slogan. Humans crave the taste of salt probably because at one time it was important to our survival, but we don't need much, and in nature food does not carry the amount of salt that processed food does today. The salt content in food is measured in milligrams (mg) of sodium. Celery is considered a high-salt vegetable—one stalk of celery contains 35 mg of sodium. But 1 ounce of potato chips carries almost five times that amount, or 168 mg; 1 ounce of pretzels carries 486 mg of sodium; 1 ounce corn chips 179 mg; 1 ounce tortilla chips 150 mg. You can see that the sodium added to food for taste is way above what nature provides and what we need, and it is the reason we finish the entire plate of nachos even after we have stopped being hungry.

The recommended intake for sodium is set at 2,400 mg daily, and it is estimated that the minimum sodium requirement for a healthy child one year of age is as little as 225 mg of sodium and an eighteen-year-old 500 mg, but Americans eat way above this at 5,000 mg, and many double that. High blood pressure is often cited as a reason to keep sodium intake low, and this is true for some individuals, but sodium may also be part of the reason Americans eat so much. We just can't resist salty food, and anyone eating a heavily processed menu will also be eating a diet high in sodium. Once again look through your child's choice of snack foods and pay attention to the sodium content. This may identify a cause of overeating.

HOW THE LOW-FAT MESSAGE MAY HAVE CONTRIBUTED TO THE OBESITY EPIDEMIC

When the term "low-fat" appears on a label it is interpreted by some to mean "eat as much as you want." This is not true. When fat is removed from a food it is replaced with carbohydrate. Gram for gram, carbohydrate carries fewer calories than fat, but it still carries calories. So a product can be fat free but not calorie free. Fat-free products such as cake, cookies, and snack food can be more troublesome to families than the original products. Everybody knows regular cake and cookies need to be consumed in moderation, but when it says "fat free" on the label it is as if the food gets a green light for being overconsumed.

Another side effect of the no-fat message occurs when people cut down on fat and eat more carbohydrate. Carbohydrate is used to replace fat in prepared food, and carbohydrate foods such as pretzels and pasta are often consumed freely because they contain no fat. In this scenario it is possible to eat a low-fat diet that is actually greater in total calories. If the low-fat message leads to an increase in more simple carbohydrates from processed foods (and the research shows that Americans are now eating 150 pounds of sugar annually, up from 120 pounds in 1970), all this excess sugar can cause insulin levels to rise, the hormone responsible for keeping blood sugar levels regulated. In the presence of chronically elevated insulin levels the body can become resistant to insulin, and this leads to type 2 diabetes.

Another downside of the low-fat message has been the inclusion and ingestion of a particular kind of fat called transunsaturated fatty acid (trans fat for short). Trans fats are produced by bubbling hydrogen through vegetable oil, making it easier and less expensive to use in processed foods and snacks. Trans fat was thought to be healthier than the saturated fat found in beef tallow or butter, and fast-food companies even switched to cooking oils containing trans fat to replace the traditional frying oils, believing it was a healthy step. Now research finds that these fats have a deleterious effect on our heart health. Trans fat can raise blood cholesterol levels as much as saturated fat, increasing the risk for heart disease, and it may be linked to childhood asthma. In a letter in the medical journal *Lancet*, Dr. Stephan Weil of the International Study of Asthma and Allergies in Childhood (ISAAC) steering committee, cites research that links the development of childhood asthma and allergies to the eating of trans fatty acids.

Trans fatty acids are found in food that contains vegetable shortening or partially hydrogenated oil. This includes most commercial snack cakes and baked goods. Food labels are not much help in determining the amount of trans fat in a food because for now they list only total fat and saturated fat. To reduce your family's intake of trans fat you will need to cook from scratch more often, using olive oil or canola oil, and use soft tub margarine, which has less trans fat than the stick type. Avoid deep-fried food, and eat a diet naturally low in fat—the lower your total fat intake the less trans fat you'll eat too.

Reshape Your Child's Food Environment

The case for eating real food is a strong one. If you embrace it and make it the foundation of food and meal choices you will find that struggles around food dissipate. If you believe serving your children good food will make them healthier you'll find it very difficult to buy or allow your kids to eat food that is not wholesome. In chapter 6 you'll find comprehensive advice on food to serve your child. This does not mean your child or family can't enjoy cake, candy, cookies, or soda. What I am asking you to take on is to be more thoughtful about your food choices and meal selections. The reason our children have become overweight is because their food environment has changed. To reverse this weight trend we need to reinstate a simpler food environment. Get back to basics, move toward a less processed, sugar-laden menu. Cook more at home, where you can control the type of fat and sugars used, or carefully purchase prepared food that is rich in nutrients and low in added sugar and salt. If you do this and establish simple family rules, such as regular meals, planned snacks, and daily exercise your child will automatically be on a diet that will bring him to his natural weight.

6

≡

The Real Food Diet

I was so embarrassed. My son's preschool sent home a note early in the year asking parents not to send candy for snacks. Today, when I picked him up, he said they wouldn't let him eat his fruit roll-up, that it was really candy. It's not like I buy the cheap stuff, it's made with real fruit."

—MOTHER OF A FOUR-YEAR-OLD BOY

Despite increasing prosperity, teens today are at high risk for poor nutrition.

—TALKING WITH TEENS: THE YMCA PARENT AND TEEN SURVEY

You know from earlier chapters that becoming overinvolved in what your child eats and restricting your child's food intake can backfire by causing weight gain and disordered eating, and can even damage the relationship between parent and child. So how can you help your child reach his natural weight without being inappropriately involved? By being involved in those areas where your involvement is essential and appropriate. These areas include: shopping, scheduling meals, planning snacks, and establishing family rules about behavior at the table.

To put your child on a diet that will help her reach her natural weight you must make real food readily available. On the following pages, you will find suggestions for Everyday choices, Sometime choices, and Occasional choices. The foods listed as Everyday choices are examples of minimally processed, real food. These are the foods you and your child should eat every day. Foods carried in the Sometime choices are more refined, have added salt and sugar or are higher in fat than the Everyday choices. Foods in the Occasional choices are processed, carry less nutrition and more calories, and are often the foods kids can't regulate well.

Review these food groups with your child and family, explain that your family will be using them as a guide to keep well nourished and healthy. Explain to your child that this is not punishment, but is an example of how you choose to show love for yourself and your family by ensuring everyone's good health. There are no forbidden foods either. Your child can eat anything; however, good nutrition will determine the foods purchased and served most often. Your child will do best if she eats three meals, and selects snacks from a list you've decided on together. On most days, each child must be served the foods he needs from each food group. At a minimum that is:

two	fruits
three	vegetables
six	grain/starch
two–three	calcium
two	protein

There is not a hard-and-fast rule for how often to eat Sometime and Occasional choices. To start, I recommend you use these foods half as much as you use them now. For example, if you are serving french fries (a vegetable placed in the Occasional choice) four times a week, reduce that to twice a week. Another way to use this system is to think of the foods in the Everyday choices as foods that can be served seven days a week, Sometime choices three times per week, and Occasional choices once per week. Of course you must use common sense. If you serve a variety of food but most of it comes from the Sometime and Occasional choices your child's overall menu will not be made up of food that will help him reach his natural weight. You can use the food records you will complete in the next chapter to assess how often Sometime and Occasional choices are served in your menu. You can also think back on or look at old grocery lists: if you are regularly buying chips, juice drinks, boxes of granola or cereal bars, creme-filled cookies, or commercially made muffins you may have identified some of the foods that are causing your child to overeat. Again this does not mean your child can't have a chip or a cookie, it just means they need to be eaten occasionally, not every day.

WHAT ABOUT CALORIES?

Counting calories is rarely a worthwhile tool, but there are things parents and children should know about caloric needs. A calorie is a unit that measures how much energy a food will provide to the body. Everybody needs calories.

The number of calories anyone needs is dependent upon activity and energy expended, body size, and health (see Recommended Energy Needs for Healthy Children). Children require additional energy for growth. At about age ten, boys start to need more calories than girls, taller children need more food than shorter kids. If energy intake is consistently greater than one needs, the extra calories are stored as body fat. If this imbalance continues, an increase in total body weight or body composition will occur.

People burn calories while resting, as well as when active. It even takes calories to burn calories; about 5 to 10 percent of the total calories we eat is used to metabolize food. Age, sex, body size, genes, physiology, even climate affect energy needs. Energy requirements can be estimated but not with great precision outside of a research lab.

RECOMMENDED ENERGY NEEDS
FOR HEALTHY CHILDREN

This is a rough estimate established by the National Research Council. Active, big kids will need more calories, smaller sedentary kids fewer calories.

Children	1–3	1,300
	4–6	1,800
	7–10	2,000
Boys	11–14	2,500
	15–18	3,000
Girls	11–18	2,200

If your health care provider has identified your child as being overweight, and there is no medical explanation, then it is a matter of too many calories in and not enough calories used in the form of activity. This means your child is out of balance. To get him back on track you need to offer your child the food he requires from the major food groups and make thoughtful decisions about snacks and desserts. You will also need to evaluate your child's level of activity.

How Much Fat Does My Child Need?

Like counting calories, keeping track of grams of fat is only part of the story. It is quite possible to have a fat-free food loaded with calories but marginal in nutrition. The focus should be on real, naturally low-fat food. Nevertheless, here is a rough guideline:

Total Calories	30 Percent of Calories in Grams of Fat
1,800 calories	66
2,000 calories	74
2,500 calories	83

The 30 percent recommended fat intake by calorie level is not an amount you must strive for. It is an amount of fat easily consumed in the course of eating a healthful diet. A child who eats a menu similar to the sample and uses food in the fat/oil group moderately will be eating a low-fat menu. (The fat/oil group is one of six food groups needed to create a balanced diet. A detailed explanation of each group begins on page 111). Each teaspoon of butter on toast, tablespoon of mayonnaise in a sandwich, or dressing on salad will add extra grams of fat to the menu. Fat can add up quickly, but it can also be enjoyed just like any other food group. Focus on getting the recommended servings from the other five food groups and use foods in the fat/oil group for cooking, to enhance flavor, and to round off appetites.

HOW MUCH PROTEIN DOES MY CHILD NEED?

Parents often worry about their children not getting enough protein, particularly if they do not eat meat. Protein does come from meat, but it is also abundant in grains, bread, beans, nuts, and all dairy products. Most healthy American children exceed their requirement for protein. The National Research Council recommends the following intake for healthy children:

	Age	Protein in Grams
Children	1–3	16
	4–6	24
	7–10	28
Boys	11–14	45
	15–18	59
Girls	11–14	46
	15–18	44

HOW MUCH SHOULD I LET MY CHILD EAT?

Let your child eat as much as he needs to satisfy his hunger. He will be able to self-regulate if he has an eating schedule

and access to good, wholesome food, food listed in the
Everyday choices. If he is frequently served food from the
Sometime and Occasional choices, such as spareribs or
french fries or sweetened cereal or cheese curls or fruit
drinks, he will not be able to self-regulate. This is the reason
you must help your child by serving the food that he can
control himself. When your child asks, "Can I have something
to eat?" don't answer yes or no. Ask her if she is hungry. If she
answers yes, then she should eat, choosing a food from the
meal, if it is about to be served, or from your list of pre-
planned snacks or from the Everyday choices in the
grain/starch, fruit, or vegetable groups. A detailed description
of each food begins on page 111. If you have been in the
habit of controlling your child's portions and food choices,
giving up control may seem unnatural at first, but over time
both you and your child will get use to this change.

How to Help Your Child Eat a Healthy Low-Fat Diet

Several studies identify high-fat diets as a cause of weight
gain. In one small study of fifteen children, ages three to
seven, the children with the highest increase in percentage body fat were found to eat a diet with a higher percentage of calories coming from fat. What's interesting
about this small study is that the fatter children were just
as active as their leaner counterparts. This suggests that
for some children, a healthy, low-fat diet and not exercise
alone will be the key to reaching their natural weight. To
put your child on a healthy low-fat diet don't drive your
child or family crazy by counting grams of fat. Instead
choose foods from the Everyday choices that follow, cook
with or add as little fat as possible to food, and serve the

recommended number of foods from each food group every day. Serve baked, broiled, or steamed food instead of fried, and limit the serving of fried food to once per week—if at all.

YOUNG KIDS, FOOD, TASTE, AND DEVELOPMENT

Remember, children do not eat like adults. They tend to like ground beef and luncheon meats over most other meats. They generally like cereal better than adults do and are less likely to eat salad, but they often like fruit and particularly juice. Between the ages of twelve to thirty-six months kids appear to be particularly "picky" about what they eat. This is so common that it is probably part of normal development. Particularly during the second year of life young children change their mind about what they like to eat. At this age don't offer too many choices; it can be too hard for your child to make decisions.

By age fifteen months a child can eat the same foods as the rest of the family, and it is at this age that children can start making demands for the foods they prefer or find most familiar. Try to serve something you know your child will like with every meal (this holds true for older kids too) such as bread or pasta. If your child won't eat what everyone else is eating, be brave enough to leave him alone and trust him to make up for it at the next meal or scheduled snack.

Remember that if all you give your child is macaroni and cheese (or canned spaghetti, hot dogs, peanut butter and jelly) he will only eat those foods. I know many preteens who eat a very limited menu because they were never encouraged to practice the One-Bite Rule when younger. I also know of young children (six and seven) who have become very overweight simply because they are offered only favorite foods and because they like these foods so much they consume way more than they would if they were eating a more varied menu.

By ages two and three a child can be encouraged to stay at the table for socializing, but you have to be prepared to give her attention—she can't sit there like a little lady quite yet, at least not for long. Around age four children want to please their parents. They will feel bad if they can't "clean their plate," if that is what you are asking them to do, so be careful about what you ask of them. Remember too that it can be normal to eat heavily at one meal and less at another.

SUGGESTED FAMILY MEAL SCHEDULE FOR GOOD NUTRITION

This is a sample meal schedule for children designed to meet the nutrition needs of children ages four to six. Children under age four can have the same variety but smaller portions (about two-thirds of a regular portion or one tablespoon from each food group for each year of life). Children over age six as well as older children, teens, and adults can have larger portions of the grain/starch, vegetable, and fruit groups. Serve the recommended servings of food from the calcium group, but increasing servings from the protein group is unnecessary. There are no recommended servings from the fat/oil group; include this group in moderation for flavor. The goal for each family is to serve the minimum number of food servings from each food group daily. To satisfy hunger, second portions from the fruit, vegetable, and grain/starch groups should be offered.

Food Group	Sample
Breakfast	
1 fruit	¾ cup juice
1 grain/starch	1 slice toast
½ calcium	½ cup milk
Midmorning snack	
1 grain/starch	2 graham crackers
½ calcium	½ cup milk
Lunch	
1 protein	2–3 ounces meat, chicken, fish, or 2 ounces cheese
1 grain/starch	½ cup macaroni
1 vegetable	3 carrot sticks
1 fruit	½ cup fruit salad
½ calcium	½ cup yogurt

Midafternoon snack

1 grain/starch	10 animal crackers
1 cup water	Free

Dinner

1 protein	2–3 ounces meat, fish or chicken, ½ cup cooked beans
1 vegetable	1 small baked potato
1 vegetable	½ cup broccoli
1 grain/starch	1 small whole wheat roll
½ calcium	½ cup milk

Minimum Total Food Groups

2 fruit

3 vegetable

6 grain/starch

2 protein (4 to 6 ounces)

2–3 calcium

HOW TO USE THE FAMILY MEAL SCHEDULE

The meal schedule is a reference tool for you to use. Young kids often need between-meal snacks, but a junior high school student may not have time to eat a midmorning snack and would do best if he ate a bigger breakfast. Arrange meals to fit your schedule, but aim to serve all the recommended food groups each day of the week. The point of a schedule is to ensure that your child (and entire family) has access to all the food they need throughout the day. A regular meal schedule will prevent extreme ranges in hunger, which can lead to overeating. It also promotes a sense of security in younger children.

WHY ARE THERE NO RECOMMENDED FOODS FROM THE FAT/OIL GROUP AND THE SNACK/SWEET/OTHER GROUP?

These groups are actually a collection of foods that can become a source of empty calories. Your child does need some servings from the fat/oil group (about three servings of added fat/oil per day and usually not more than six), to obtain the essential fatty acids these foods carry. Children obtain additional fat when they eat food prepared with cooking oils; when they put a dressing on a salad; or eat a handful of nuts as a snack; or eat prepared foods like bread, muffins, and cookies that naturally carry fat. High-fat fried food or food served with large amounts of added fat in the form of butter, mayonnaise, or salad dressing should be served in moderation.

Many of the food items in the snack/sweet/other group carry a lot of calories and little nutrition. This food group does not carry any nutrients that can't be found in one of the other food groups. However, many foods listed here taste delicious and you wouldn't want to eliminate them entirely. In general use foods from the snack/sweet/other group "sparingly" and rely on the other food groups for nutrition.

EVERYDAY SNACK SUGGESTIONS

Any food from the following Everyday choices in the fruit and the vegetable groups can be eaten as a snack whenever hungry. Offer Everyday choices from the grain/starch group as the next best choice. Everyday choices from the calcium and protein groups can be served as snacks, but count these servings toward the day's total. When children eat more than two to three servings from the calcium or protein groups they tend to replace food from other food groups.

Vegetables: carrot sticks, sliced cucumbers, garden tomatoes, peppers, veggies and dip.

Fruits: cantaloupe, orange slices, melon balls, berries, grapes, fruit salad, fruit kabobs.

Grains/starches: bagel crisps, crisp breadsticks, raisin bread, graham crackers, pretzels, plain rice cakes, popcorn cakes, saltine-type crackers, whole wheat crackers, animal crackers, fortune cookies, fig bars, gingersnaps, Cheerios, Wheaties, or any whole grain, low-sugar cereal, salsa with baked crackers or baked chips, homemade whole grain muffins.

Calcium: low-fat yogurt, frozen yogurt, or hot cocoa made with low-fat milk.

WHAT ABOUT DESSERTS?

You might think that when weight loss is the goal, desserts should go out the window. That is an unrealistic approach for children. Instead, decide how dessert fits for your child. Most children can afford the three hundred calories that a typical dessert, in the Sometime and even Occasional choices, carries. The problem today is that many items our children perceive as snack food, such as a cereal bar or a fruit drink, carry sugar value equivalent to cookies and soda. As a result our children eat a lot of food that ought to be called dessert but isn't.

What I like about cupcakes, cookies, and candy is that these are honest desserts, and every child in America knows his mom and dad are not going to let him eat dessert without some restriction. For this reason dessert is usually not the source of unnatural weight gain. In fact, you should serve dessert so your child doesn't feel deprived.

HOW MUCH DESSERT SHOULD A CHILD HAVE?

Because older children can afford the three hundred calories in an honest dessert I'd say most children can eat the dessert of their choice three times per week, very active kids can eat it daily. There is nothing wrong with dessert, the only problem with cake, ice cream, and cookies is that they do not carry the leader nutrients your child needs for growth. If a child eats a lot of this food they won't have room to eat the food their body really needs to fight disease and promote optimal growth. This is particularly true for children under age four, who may eat only 1,200 to 1,400 calories in a day. One dessert can represent 20 percent to 30 percent of their day's intake. On most days you want to serve your child the minimum number of recommended servings from each food group. On occasion select a dessert to replace a serving of fruit or just add it to the day's meal. Read more about how to handle dessert on page 259 under Questions and Answers. Also see Healthful Desserts.

HEALTHFUL DESSERTS

When you serve dessert why not make it rich in nutrition? Any of the following recipes, included in chapter 8, make great choices.

Blackened Banana

Fruit Crumble

Fruit Clafouti

Baked Apples

Apple Soufflé

Peanut Butter Cupcakes

Fruit Salad

Pumpkin Pudding

Applesauce Cake

Blueberry Grunt

Poached Peaches or Pears

Meringue Cookies

YOU'VE ELIMINATED SOME OF OUR FAVORITE FOODS!

When you read through my recommendations for Everyday choices you may find that some of your child's favorite foods are placed with the Sometime and Occasional choices. Foods are placed in these groups because they carry less nutrition or the food is one that kids tend to overconsume because of its fat, sugar, or salt content. You as the adult get to make the final decision about what your child is to eat. I am presenting you with recommendations that I hope will make the task easier. Only you know what will work in your family.

If some of my advice does not "fit" for you or your family then do not use it. The purpose of developing the food lists that follow is to provide you with as concrete and specific a resource as possible without actually telling you what to eat every day. Nothing will replace your child's need for good nutrition, but being thoughtful and conscientious about what you eat is as important as good nutrition. Trying my suggestions and finding they don't all work for you is being thoughtful and conscientious.

HOW ARE THE FOOD GROUPS DETERMINED?

There are over forty essential nutrients and thousands of naturally occurring chemicals that are needed to maintain health. It is impossible to keep track of all these nutrients, and it would take all the fun out of eating if you did. To make the task of eating well reasonably uncomplicated dietitians divide foods into six food groups. The U.S. Department of Agriculture developed the Food Guide Pyramid as a graphic representation of these food groups. These food groups include fruit, vegetable, protein, calcium, grain/starch, and fat/oil, snack/sweet/other. Each of these groups is a good source of one or more leader nutrients. Leader nutrients are the nutrients we need in large amounts. They include protein, carbohydrates, fat, fiber, calcium, vitamins A, E, C, and iron. Food that is a good source of leader nutrients also carries the nutrients we need in smaller amounts, called the secondary nutrients. By encouraging your child to eat the recommended servings from all the food groups he will be well nourished.

Preceding each food list you'll find an approximate nutrition content per serving. The food listed in the Everyday food choices is food that best fits this nutrition profile and is a good source of the essential leader nutrients. Food in the Occasional list is placed here either because it doesn't fit the nutrient profile, it carries only some essential nutri-

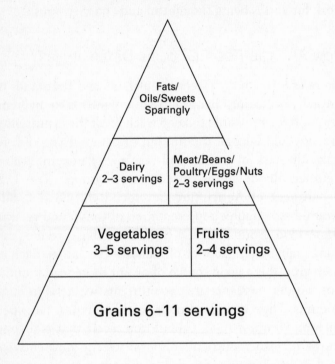

The USDA Food Guide Pyramid
A Guide to Daily Food Choices

ents, or it is a food kids tend to overeat. For example, avocado is in the Occasional choice of the fruit group because
it carries more fat than fruit typically does. Relish and pickles are in the Occasional choice of the vegetable section not
because they are high in calories but because they are low in

nutrition (I don't want any family to get the idea that relish can be counted as a serving of vegetables).

Some food will straddle two groups, for instance beans can count as a protein and a grain/starch because it is a good source of carbohydrate and protein. Cheese is in the protein group and calcium group because it carries both calcium and protein. Nuts contain both protein and fat and can be found in the protein and fat/oil groups. In the end these are guides. Use them as tools to help you understand where the real foods can be found and to plan meals and shopping lists, but don't be an absolute slave to them either.

FIVE ESSENTIAL FOOD STRATEGIES TO HELP YOUR CHILD REACH HIS NATURAL WEIGHT

To put your child on a healthy diet that will lead him toward his natural weight you will need to practice these five steps:

1. Follow the basic meal schedule guidelines on pages 98 through 100. This will give you a structure to meet your child's need for nutrition.
2. Make a list of acceptable between-meal snacks (use my list or make your own). When hungry serve snacks or second portions from the Everyday choices of the fruit, vegetable, and grain/starch groups.
3. Become familiar with the Everyday choices in each food group.
4. Shop from a grocery list that includes mostly Everyday choices. See a sample grocery list on page 202.
5. Know how many servings you and your child need from each food group.

LEADER AND SECONDARY NUTRIENTS AND WHAT THEY DO

Leader Nutrients

Protein: Builds and repairs tissue, such as skin and muscles. Part of antibodies that fight disease; helps make enzymes to aid digestion.

Calcium: Keeps bones and teeth healthy. Assists in muscle contraction and blood clotting.

Fat: Provides energy and carries essential fatty acids and fat-soluble vitamins; insulates and pads the body.

Carbohydrate: Supplies energy; spares protein from being used as an energy source so it can be used for more important tasks such as healing.

Vitamin A: Helps with good vision, skin, and mucous membranes. Involved in the making of essential hormones.

Vitamin E: Helps prevent cell damage; protects red blood cells and skin.

Vitamin C: Helps keep blood vessels strong; important in the making of scar tissue, metabolizing protein, boosting the immune system, and in the absorption of iron.

Iron: Carries oxygen throughout the body as part of red blood cells.

Secondary Nutrients

Thiamin: Important in energy production, appetite, and to the nervous system.

Riboflavin: Assists in energy metabolism and keeps skin and eyes healthy.

Niacin: Helps in the release of energy; important

to the proper functioning of the nervous and digestive system and to the skin.

Folate: Essential to the making of new cells.

Vitamin B12: Needed to make new cells and keep nerve cells healthy.

Biotin: Needed for the metabolism of energy, fat production, and the use of amino acids.

Pantothenic acid: Helps metabolize carbohydrates, protein, and fat.

Pyridoxine: Needed in the metabolism of protein and the proper use of carbohydrate.

Vitamin D: Vital for strong bones and teeth.

Vitamin K: Essential to proper blood clotting.

Potassium: Helps maintain fluid balance in cells and in muscle contraction.

Phosphorous: Needed to keep bones and teeth healthy.

Magnesium: Helps build protein, keeps muscles and teeth strong.

Zinc: Needed in wound healing and for a healthy sense of taste.

Iodine: Prevents goiter, makes up part of thyroid hormone.

Copper: Vital to proper iron absorption, makes up part of the membrane that covers and protects nerve tissue.

Manganese: Part of the enzymes that are needed for the healthy functioning of cells.

Chromium: Needed for the proper release of stored energy.

Selenium: Works with vitamin E to prevent important body compounds from being destroyed.

Molybdenum: Needed by several enzymes to ensure proper cell functioning.

NUTRIENTS CONTAINED
IN EACH FOOD GROUP

Each food group carries a specific profile of nutrients, which are listed below. To obtain a good balance of nutrients, food from all the food groups must be consumed regularly. This is why a "balanced" diet is recommended for good health. It is important for both kids and parents to understand why eating from all these food groups is important.

VEGETABLE

Vegetables contain vitamins E, A, and C, carbohydrates, calcium (green leafy vegetables), as well as vitamin K, folate, magnesium, and potassium. A good source of fiber.

FRUIT

Fruit will carry vitamins A and C, carbohydrates, vitamin K, and potassium. Good source of fiber.

GRAIN/STARCH

Starchy foods such as breads, rice, and cereal will provide carbohydrates, iron (in fortified food), chromium (in wheat germ and whole grains), thiamin, riboflavin, niacin, vitamin B6, biotin, manganese (whole grains), and panthothenic acid. A good source of fiber.

CALCIUM

Food in this group is the best source of calcium, and some are also a good source of protein (dairy foods), vitamins A, K, D, and B12, phosphorus, molybdenum.

PROTEIN

All foods in this group, whether from animal or vegetable sources, contain protein; most are a good source of iron. Secondary nutrients in this group include: vitamins A, B12, B6, D (eggs), and K (meat and eggs), biotin, riboflavin, pantothenic acid, niacin, phosphorus, copper, iodine (fish), selenium, zinc.

FAT/OIL

Nuts and oils provide fat, vitamin E, vitamin D, magnesium (whole seeds), copper (nuts and seeds).

SNACK/SWEET/OTHER

Food in this group is not recommended as a source of leader and secondary nutrients because though they contain some nutrition they are usually very dense in calories.

VEGETABLE GROUP

Offer your child at least three servings of vegetables every day. Try to serve a variety of choices, but if raw carrots are a favorite—go with it. Serve vegetables raw or cooked. Baked, steamed, stir-fried are all good cooking methods.

For convenience buy canned (try low-sodium) or frozen plain vegetables, packaged salad, cut up; carrots and celery, salad, and vegetables from the salad bar that are not marinated. Vegetables served in cooked foods such as casseroles and soup count too. If your child "hates" vegetables practice the One-Bite Rule and serve extra portions of fruit to make up for the missed consumption of vegetables.

A serving of vegetables should contain approximately 25 calories, 1 g protein, 0 to 2 g fat, 6 g carbohydrate, 2 g fiber, 400+ RE vitamin A, 6+ mg vitamin C, 0.7 mg vitamin E. They also carry fewer than 50 grams of sodium, 200 mg of potassium and the hard-to-measure naturally occurring phytochemicals that fight disease.

Suggested Serving Size

(If these serving sizes seem too large for youngsters, start with a tablespoon and work up.)

1 cup leafy vegetables

½ cup cooked or cut-up vegetables

½ cup tomato or vegetable juice or soup

Everyday Choices

Artichoke, asparagus, beans (green, wax, Italian), bean sprouts, beets, broccoli, brussels sprouts, cabbage, carrots, cauliflower, celery, corn (plain or cream style), cucumber, eggplant, green onion or scallions, greens (collard, kale, mustard, turnip), kelp, kohlrabi, leeks, lima beans, mixed vegetables, mushrooms, okra, onions, peas, pea pods, peppers (all varieties), potato, radishes, salad greens (endive,

escarole, lettuce, romaine, spinach), spinach, summer
squash, tomato, tomato/vegetable juice, turnips, water
chestnuts, watercress, zucchini. Homemade vegetable
soup including cream soup made with low-fat milk.

Sometime Choices

Canned vegetable soup; frozen vegetables (any type) with
light sauce (less than 5 g fat/serving); potatoes: instant
mashed, mashed, O'Brien, stuffed; sauerkraut; tomato
sauce and spaghetti sauce (high in sodium).

Occasional Choices

Canned cream of vegetable soup; coleslaw; french fries;
fried vegetables; frozen vegetables with cheese, butter, or
cream sauce (more than 5 g fat per serving); hashed
brown potatoes, potatoes au gratin, potato chips, potato
salad, scalloped potatoes, shoestring potatoes, Tater Tots.

Olives are placed in with other fats; pickles and relish
are not high enough in nutrients to count as a good vegetable choice, but they are not high in calories either and
can be used to add flavor to your child's food.

FRUIT GROUP

Most children enjoy fruit and juice and will have no trouble consuming the recommended two servings every day.
I encourage whole fruit over juice because it takes longer
to eat; it might take eight minutes to eat an apple and
only eight seconds to drink a glass of apple juice.

For convenience buy frozen or canned fruits or juices

without added sugar. Frozen juice concentrates maintain their nutrition when reconstituted; canned fruits lose their peels, but they still carry essential nutrients. Food companies know parents want to serve their children real fruit, so they add statements like "made with real fruit" to food labels—be wary. In one popular apple cereal bar your child would have to eat seventy bars to eat the equivalent of one whole apple!

A serving of real fruit should roughly provide your child with 70 calories, 1 g protein, 0 g fat, 15 g carbohydrate, 1 to 2 g fiber, 32+ RE vitamin A, 35+ mg vitamin C, less than 10 mg of sodium, and more than 250 mg of potassium.

Suggested Serving Size

Notice the serving of juice is 6 ounces not the 8 or 12 that comes in many ready-to-serve containers.

1 medium piece fruit

½ cup cut or cooked fruit

¼ cup dried fruit

¾ cup fruit juice

Everyday Choices

Apple, applesauce, apricots, banana, blackberries, blueberries, cantaloupe, carambola, cherimoya, cherries, cranberries (raw), dates, figs, fruit cocktail, fruit salad, grapefruit, grapes, honeydew melon, kiwifruit, mandarin oranges, mango, nectarine, orange, papaya, peach, pear, pineapple, plum, prunes, raisins, raspberries, strawberries, tangerines, watermelon. Canned fruit packed in fruit juice.

Juices

Apple juice with vitamin C, grapefruit juice, orange juice, pineapple juice, prune juice.

Sometime Choices

Apple cider, apricot nectar, papaya nectar, peach nectar, pear nectar, cranberry sauce, 100 percent fruit juice blends, canned fruit packed in light syrup, cranberry juice, grape juice.

Occasional Choices

Avocado (high in fat but still a good source of nutrition); fruit canned in heavy syrup; fruit drink, punch, or ade (see fruit drinks listed in Liquid Candy, page 134); fruit bars; fruit rolls.

IS IT A WHOLE GRAIN FOOD?

Selecting a food that is truly whole grain can be difficult. It seems that some companies actually try to confuse consumers with food coloring added to make white bread and crackers look like whole grain and with labels that say "wheat flour," suggesting it is the same as whole wheat flour, which it is not. A whole grain food must list one of the following first on its list of ingredients: brown rice, bulgur, cracked wheat, graham flour, oatmeal, popcorn, whole barley, whole cornmeal, whole oats, whole rye, whole wheat. Ingredients such as wheat flour, enriched flour, and degerminated cornmeal are not whole grains.

GRAIN/STARCH GROUP

Each family member requires six servings (or more) from this group to obtain the carbohydrates they need for energy and the B vitamins to use it. The more active the individual the more food needed from this group. Very active teen boys, for example, may need as much as eleven or twelve servings from this group daily. This food group is also likely to be the second largest source of protein in your family's diet. In general, foods in this group are low in fat but often served with fat added, such as butter on bread, cream cheese on a bagel. Most of these foods are fortified with iron, an essential nutrient for young kids. These foods are your only source of the cereal fiber that research shows can fight disease and control appetite. I recommend adults strive for at least three whole grain foods daily and offer young children at least one serving of whole grain food every day. Whole grain cereals are an easy way to accomplish this. Each serving of food from this group should contain approximately 80 to 100 calories, 2 g protein, 0 to 4 g fat, 15 g carbohydrate, 1 to 3 g fiber, 0.1 mg vitamin E, 1 mg iron, and roughly 150 to 200 mg sodium per serving.

Suggested Serving Size

1 slice bread

½ small bagel, English muffin, pita bread, or bun

4 to 6 crackers

½ cup cooked cereal, pasta, rice, or other grain

¾ cup dry cereal

½ cup cooked beans, lentils, peas, potato, or winter squash

Everyday Choices

Bread

Bagel, bread (white, whole wheat, pumpernickel, rye), breadsticks (crisp), English muffin, hot dog or hamburger roll, pita, raisin bread, rolls (white or whole grain), tortilla (soft corn or flour).

Cereal

There is a huge selection of cereal to chose from. Take the time to find one that gives your child the most nutrition. Look for cereal, cooked or ready to eat, that carries less than 10 g of sugar and 3 or more grams of fiber per serving. AllBran (Kellogg's), Bran Buds, bran flakes, Cheerios (Gen Mills), Crunchy Bran (Quaker), Fiber One (Gen Mills), Fruit Wheats (Nabisco), Golden Multigrain Flakes (Healthy Choice), Grape-Nut Flakes (Post), Grape-Nuts (Post), Multi Grain Cheerios (Gen Mills), oat bran, Oatmeal Squares (Quaker), Raisin Bran, shredded wheat, Shredded Wheat Squares (Kellogg's), Total (Gen Mills), Wheaties (Gen Mills).

Cooked Cereal

Cream of rye (Roman Meal), Maypo, oatmeal (plain), Wheatena, Whole Wheat Natural (Quaker).

Crackers and Snacks

Animal crackers, bagel chips, crisp bread, flat bread, graham crackers, matzoh, melba toast, milk crackers, whole grain homemade muffins, whole grain muffins from mix (no hydrogenated or partially hydrogenated fat added), oyster crackers, popcorn (air popped or low-fat microwave), pretzels, plain rice cakes, popcorn cakes, saltine-type crackers, whole wheat crackers (no fat added), zwieback cracker.

Grains

Barley, buckwheat, bulgur, cornmeal, couscous, flour (dry), grits, kasha, millet, noodles, oats, pasta, potato (if served to replace a starch), wonton wrappers, quinoa, rice (white, brown, or wild), wheat berries, wheat germ. Rice or noodle soup.

Beans, Peas, and Lentils

Black beans, garbanzo beans, pinto, kidney, white, split, black-eyed lentils, miso, soup made from any of these foods.

Sometime Choices

Bread

One ounce carries more than 4 g fat and/or fewer than 2 g fiber. Biscuit (homemade and commercial), breadstick (soft from refrigerated dough), corn bread, muffin (home-made with white flour), pancakes, quick breads: apple, banana, blueberry, carrot, cranberry, pumpkin.

Cereal

Cereals placed here contain 3 g or less of cereal fiber per serving, or more than 2 g of fat or more than 10 g of sugar. Apple Raisin Crisp (Kellogg's), Basic 4 (Gen Mills), Branola (Post), cornflakes (low in fiber), Crispix (Kellogg's), crispy rice, Frosted Mini-Wheats (Kellogg's), Fruit & Fiber (Post), granola, Honey Bunches of Oats (Post), Honey Nut Cheerios (Gen Mills), Honeycomb (Post), Kaboom (Gen Mills), Kix (Gen Mills), Life (Quaker), muesli, Oatmeal Crisp (Gen Mills), Product 19 (Kellogg's), puffed rice or wheat cereal, Special K (Kellogg's).

Cooked Cereal

Contains less than 3 g fiber, and/or more than 10 g sugar per serving. Banana Nut Multigrain instant (Nabisco), corn grits, Cream of Wheat (reg flavor), Farina, Oatmeal instant (flavored).

Crackers/Snacks

Cake and cupcakes with low-fat frosting, cookies, croutons, flavored rice cakes, granola bars, popcorn (commercially popped).

Grains, Beans, Peas, and Lentils

Canned spaghetti w/sauce, macaroni salad.
Baked beans with pork, refried beans made with lard.

Occasional Choices

Bread

One ounce carries more than 6 g fat, and/or less than 1 g fiber. Corn bread, croissant, muffin (commercially made), stuffing, toaster pastry, fried tortilla, waffle.

Cereal

Cereal contains less than 1 g fiber, more than 10 g sugar, and/or more than 2 g fat per serving. Cereal from this list is best served to replace dessert, not as a breakfast cereal. Alpha-Bits (Post), Apple Cinnamon Cheerios (Gen Mills), Apple Jacks (Kellogg's), Apple Zaps (Quaker), Berry Berry Kix (Gen Mills), Blueberry Morning (Post), Body Buddies (Gen Mills), Boo Berry (Gen Mills), Cap'n Crunch (Quaker), Cinnamon Mini Buns (Kellogg's), Cinnamon Toast Crunch (Gen Mills), Cocoa Blasts (Quaker), Cocoa Krispies (Kellogg's), Cocoa Pebbles (Post), Cocoa Puffs (Gen Mills), Corn Pops (Kellogg's), Corn Quakes (Quaker), Count Chocula (Gen Mills), Cracklin Oat Bran (Kellogg's), Crispin Cracking Rice (Malt-o-Meal), Double Dip Crunch (Kellogg's), Franken Berry (Gen Mills), French Toast Crunch (Gen Mills), Froot Loops (Kellogg's), Frosted Cheerios (Gen Mills), Frosted Flakes, Frosted Krispies (Kellogg's), Frosted Rice, Fruitangy Oh!s (Quaker), Fruity Marshmallow Krispies (Kellogg's), Fruity Pebbles, Golden Crisp (Post), Golden Grahams (Gen Mills), Honey Crunch Cornflakes (Kellogg's), Honey Frosted Wheaties (Gen Mills), Honey Graham Oh's (Quaker), Honeycomb (Post), Lucky Charms (Gen Mills), Marshmallow Alpha-Bits (Post), Quisp

(Quaker), Reese's Puffs (Gen Mills), Rice Krispies Treats (Kellogg's), S'mores Grahams (Gen Mills), Smacks (Kellogg's), Sugar Corn Pops (Kellogg's), Sugar Frosted Corn Flakes (Malt-o-Meal), Sugar Frosted Flakes (Ralston Purina), Sweet Puffs (Quaker), Tootie Fruities (Malt-o-Meal), Total Corn Flakes (Gen Mills), Triples (Gen Mills), Trix (Gen Mills).

Cooked Cereal

A serving contains less than 1 g fiber and more than 10 g sugar. Cream of rice, Cream of Wheat, flavored. Maltomeal.

Crackers/Snacks

Cake and cupcake (frosted homemade or commercial), cheese balls/curls, cheese bread, chow mein noodles, corn bread, corn chips, croissant, doughnut, fried rice, granola, muffin (commercially made), pastry, pie crust, stuffing, toaster pastry, tortilla (fried), waffle.

POTATOES: STARCH OR VEGETABLE?

Potatoes are technically a vegetable, but many of us serve potatoes as a starch to replace rice or noodles. When used as a starch, count it as a serving from the grain/starch group and serve other vegetables from the vegetable group to meet your child's recommended intake of three per day.

Calcium Group

This group includes milk, yogurt, and cheese. In the first year of life breast milk is the best choice, followed by infant formula. At one year of age most pediatricians allow the introduction of whole (never low-fat) cow's milk. Start skim or 1 percent milk after your child's second birthday. Each serving from this group should carry at least 300 mg of calcium. Young children require only two servings of calcium-rich food daily, older children and adults three servings. This food group can be a significant source of unneeded calories for some children, particularly if your child is eating from the Sometime and Occasional choices most often. See the box on page 125 about calcium requirements. Calcium does not need to come from dairy products; vegetables, beans, even nuts carry calcium too. Milk is cited so often as a good source of calcium because it is so rich in this mineral and kids like it.

Each serving in this food group should carry approximately 90 calories, 8 g protein, 0 to 3 g fat, 12 g carbohydrate, 300 mg calcium, and 150 RE vitamin A.

Suggested Serving Size

1 cup milk or yogurt
1½ to 2 ounces cheese

Everyday Choices

Acidophilus milk (skim and 1 percent), buttermilk, cheese with less than 2 g fat per ounce, evaporated skim milk, farmer cheese, low-fat frozen yogurt fortified with calcium, low-fat (1 percent) milk, low-fat plain and fruited yogurt (look for yogurt with active cultures and real fruit and 30 percent calcium on the label), nonfat dry milk (reconstituted), nonfat milk, nonfat plain yogurt, Parmesan cheese, Romano cheese, skim milk.

LACTOSE INTOLERANCE

Lactose intolerance is a condition that often runs in families. It occurs when the enzyme lactase, which digests the milk sugar lactose, is lacking. Symptoms include abdominal pain, flatulence, a bloated feeling, cramps, and diarrhea. The more lactose a child consumes the greater the symptoms. Once a lactose intolerance is identified all lactose-containing foods should be avoided until symptoms subside. A child may be able to tolerate small amounts of lactose when consumed as part of a meal, but ask your doctor. If the problem runs in your family you may want to ask about avoiding or limiting foods that contain lactose. Lactose-containing foods include: all types of milk (and products made from milk), cheese, creamed soup, pudding, yogurt, mixed dishes made with cheese or milk, and breads and rolls made with milk. Lactose-rich foods are also rich in the essential nutrient calcium. Alternative sources of calcium include: almonds, cooked greens, oysters, rhubarb, brazil nuts, broccoli, tofu, calcium-fortified soy milk, fruit juice, and calcium-fortified ready-to-eat cereal.

Everyday Nondairy Calcium Sources

The following foods carry 300 mg of calcium per serving, but calories and protein content will vary.

Almonds (6 oz), greens (3 cups), kefir (1 cup), navy beans (2½ cups cooked), orange juice (1 cup calcium fortified), sardines (3 oz), soy milk* (1 cup calcium fortified), tofu (8 oz), rice milk* (1 cup fortified), goat's milk* (1 cup).

Sometimes Choices

Most of these foods carry more calories than plain milk and/or fewer than 300 mg of calcium per serving.

Hot chocolate (made with low-fat milk), ice milk, low-fat chocolate milk, low-fat cottage cheese, low-fat frozen yogurt, low-fat (2 percent) milk, low-fat cheese containing less than 5 grams of fat per ounce, lactose-reduced low-fat 2 percent milk, part-skim ricotta cheese, pudding made with 1 percent or skim milk, prepared Instant Breakfast.

Occasional Choices

Cheese is a good protein and calcium source, but it also carries a good deal of fat—approximately 8 or 9 g of fat per ounce, a fat content equal to that found in prime rib, butter, and cream. Two ounces of full-fat cheese can provide your child with almost 25 percent of his fat require-

---

*Nondairy milks may not contain all the vitamins and protein young children need. Discuss their use with your health care provider.

ment for the day. Most cheese products are listed as an Occasional choice, and the serving recommendation for full-fat cheese is about twice per week.

American cheese, blue cheese, brick cheese, brie cheese, Camembert cheese, cheddar cheese, imitation/ substitute cheese, cheese spread, chocolate milk (whole), Colby Cheese, condensed milk, cottage cheese (4 percent), cream cheese, custard, Edam cheese, evaporated whole milk, feta cheese, filled milk, flavored milk drinks, fontina cheese, gjetost cheese, goat cheese, Gouda cheese, Gruyère cheese, havarti cheese, hot chocolate (made with whole milk), ice cream, malted milk, Monterey Jack cheese, mozzarella cheese, Muenster cheese, Neufchâtel cheese, nondairy creamers, Port du Salut cheese, pudding made with whole milk or cream, processed cheese, provolone cheese, Roquefort cheese, sheep's milk, sour cream substitute, Swiss cheese, Tilsit cheese, whole buttermilk, whole-fat frozen yogurt, whole milk, whole-milk yogurt, whole-milk ricotta cheese.

CALCIUM REQUIREMENTS FOR CHILDREN AND YOUNG ADULTS

Children	1-3 years	500 mg
	4-8 years	800 mg
Males	9-18 years	1,300 mg
Females	9-18 years	1,300 mg

Men and women need 1,000 mg per day up to age fifty and 1,200 mg for fifty and over.

WHAT TO DO ABOUT CHEESE?

Because cheese is a favorite with many kids and it can count as both a calcium or protein choice, it can be confusing to decide how often to serve it. If your child eats cheese as a protein source, such as in a grilled cheese sandwich or macaroni and cheese as a main dish, count the cheese as a serving from the protein group not the calcium group. If your child does not drink milk but must rely on cheese as a calcium source, then count it as a serving from the calcium group.

But be aware that cheese is a high-fat, high-calorie food. When served it will provide your child with 330 calories, not the 120 to 180 calories other protein choices provide, or the 90 calories other calcium choices provide. For this reason, to keep your child on a low-fat menu, try limiting the serving of full-fat cheese to twice per week. Soy cheese is a good cow's milk cheese replacement. It is low in fat, rich in protein but not equal in calcium. Read labels. If the soy cheese does not contain calcium, then count it as a protein source and get your calcium somewhere else.

PROTEIN GROUP

This food group, which includes meat, poultry, fish, dry beans, eggs, and nuts, can be a significant source of excess calories when portions are too large or selections are very high in fat. Healthy men, women, and children require only two small servings (about 5 to 7 ounces) in a day, but many Americans eat way above this. Most young children are not tremendous meat eaters (except for hamburger) until older, but they do like the deli and sausage meats. A child does not need to eat red meat. Fish, chicken, even beans, eggs, and nuts are superb protein sources too. A serving from this group should carry approximately 120 to 180 calories, 16 to 24 g protein, 6 to 10 g fat, 1 g of carbohydrate, 1 to 2 mg iron.

Suggested Serving Size

- 2 to 3 ounces of lean meat, fish, or poultry
- ½ cup to ¾ cup tuna or cottage cheese
- 2 to 3 ounces of cheese (3 oz cheese contains 330 calories, 20 g protein, 27 g fat)
- ½ cup of cooked dry beans, 2 tbsp peanut butter, or 1 egg = 1 oz meat (Look under fats/oils for additional nut/seed choices.)

Everyday Choices

Meat

Canadian bacon, dried chipped beef, game (rabbit, venison), luncheon meats that have fewer than 4 g of fat per ounce, lean pork tenderloin, rib eye steak, sirloin, veal cutlet.

Poultry

Chicken (fresh and canned), cornish hen, ground turkey breast (fewer than 10 g of fat per 3 ounces), chicken or turkey hot dog (1), luncheon meat, turkey ham, turkey pastrami, turkey (preferably not self-basting), pheasant.

Fish

Catfish, canned seafood in water or broth (clams, shrimp, salmon, oysters, crabmeat, tuna), clams, crab, flounder, haddock, halibut, imitation crabmeat, lobster, mussels, ocean perch, oysters, pollack, rockfish, salmon, scallops, shrimp, sole, trout, whiting.

Dry Beans, Eggs, Nuts, Tofu

Black-eyed peas, chickpeas, egg, egg substitute, hot dog, tofu, kidney beans, lentils, mung beans, navy beans, northern beans, pinto beans, refried beans (made without lard), seeds and nuts (1 tbsp), peanut butter, almonds or cashew butter, soybeans, split peas, tofu, vegetarian burger (1 patty).

Sometime Choices

Meat

Beef jerky, beef tenderloin, chuck roast, flank steak, ground beef (extra lean), hot dog (1), kielbasa (low-fat), liver, lamb, pork chop, pork roast, prime rib.

Poultry

Goose, ground turkey.

Fish

Mackerel, prebreaded fish.

Dry Beans, Eggs, Nuts, Tofu

Bean dip (with added fat), seeds.

Occasional Choices

Meat

Bacon, bologna, corned beef, ground beef, Lunchables, liverwurst, porterhouse steak, rib roast, ribs, salt pork, sausage, short ribs, spareribs, T-bone steak, veal breast.

Poultry

Fried chicken, frozen fried, or breaded chicken.

Fish

Fried fish, prepared seafood salad, tuna in oil, fish or clam chowders made with cream.

Dry Beans, Eggs, Nuts, Tofu

Nuts.

FAT/OIL GROUP

Small amounts of fat in the form of vegetable oil such as canola and olive oil should be included in the family menu. They carry the essential fatty acid known as linoleic acid. We also obtain fat from dairy products, meat, baked goods, and in any food prepared with fat. Fat in the form of butter, soft margarine, salad dressing, and mayonnaise tastes good and enhances the flavor of food, making meals more enjoyable.

The following suggestions will maintain the family's fat intake at a healthy level: keep your intake of fried foods to once per week (if at all) and use as little oil, butter, or margarine in cooking as possible. Try to keep the servings individual family members add to food (such as margarine on toast or dressing on salad) to three per day and not more than six. Three servings of the Everyday choices below will add only 15 grams of fat to your menu for the day and provide you with the essential fatty acids you need. Teach your family to be thoughtful about this food group, but don't eliminate it either.

One serving from this group will carry about 45 calories and 5 g of fat and small but important amounts of vitamin E. Canola oil carries about 3 mg per tbsp of vitamin E, olive oil 2 mg, sunflower oil 7 mg, sunflower seeds 14 mg per ounce, and 1 tbsp Italian dressing 1.5 mg of vitamin E. Children and adults require 6 to 10 mg of vitamin E daily.

Suggested Serving Size

1 tsp unsaturated oil, margarine, or butter

1 tbsp salad dressing, mayonnaise

1 tbsp seeds and nuts

Everyday Choices

Unsaturated oils (including canola, corn, olive, peanut, safflower, sesame, or soybean oil), walnut oil, vegetable oil spray, soft or liquid margarine, low-fat mayonnaise, butter (soft spread), salad dressings made with the above oils. Almonds, peanuts, sunflower seeds.

Sometime Choices

Butter, stick margarine, tartar sauce.

Occasional Choices

Bacon, chitterlings, coconut, cream, fatback or salt pork, palm or palm kernel oil, shortening or lard, sour cream.

SNACKS/SWEETS/OTHER GROUP

Kids will love to see that I have an Everyday choice for snacks and sweets, but this may not be as good as it sounds. I am not telling you to serve dessert every day, but I am saying keep the Everyday choices on hand so when you want to serve dessert you have an appropriate selection to choose from. Just because Twizzlers are under the Everyday choices for candy does not mean a child should eat candy every day. You will notice there is not a recommended daily intake for this group on my suggested meal schedule on page 98. However, if you're packing a lunch for a picnic or a bike ride or a field trip your kids will love it if they have something fun to eat. Keep your focus on eating a healthful diet over a seven-day period, and meeting your exercise goals. If you do this, your child can certainly afford the calories from this food group.

But don't keep too wide a selection of sweets and snack-type foods on hand either—kids tend to eat more when there is a greater variety to choose from. Some snack foods such as crackers are listed earlier in the grain/starch group. If you have trouble with this group, read more about handling snacks and sweets in chapter 9, Questions and Answers. Everyday, Sometime, and Occasional choices are provided for cookies, frozen desserts, baked/prepared desserts, candy, and liquid candy.

IS IT SUGAR?

Sugar is often listed by names that are unrecognizable. A food label that lists any of the following ingredients carries added sugar: Brown sugar, corn sweetner, corn syrup, dextrose, fructose, fruit juice concentrate, glucose, high-fructose corn syrup, honey, invert sugar, lactose, maltose, malt syrup, molasses, raw sugar, sucrose, syrup, table sugar.

Cookies

Everyday Choices

Each contains about 90 to 100 calories per serving, has less than 1 g of fiber, less than 3 g of fat, and 15 g of sugar: animal crackers, fig bars, fortune cookies, gingersnaps, graham crackers.

Sometime Choices

Cereal/granola bar, creme sandwich, chocolate chip, lady finger, molasses, Nilla wafer, oatmeal, Pop Tart or other toaster pastry.

Occasional Choices

Butter cookies, brownie, chocolate-covered cookies, short-bread, sugar cookies, sugar wafer.

Frozen Desserts

Everyday Choices

One serving is ½ cup, 100 calories, and has less than 3 g of fat. Ice milk, nonfat ice cream, nonfat frozen yogurt, ice pops, water ices.

Sometime Choices

Sherbert, sorbet.

Occasional Choices

Frozen pie and cake, premium ice cream, and ice cream bars.

Baked/Prepared Desserts

Everyday Choices

Angel food cake, flavored gelatin, all flavors pudding and pie filling made with 1 percent milk.

Sometime Choices

Cake and cupcakes with low-fat frosting, plain gingerbread cake, pound cake, fruit crisp.

Occasional Choices

Cheesecake, cream puff, croissant, Danish pastry, doughnut (plain or filled), fruit turnover, fruit and cream pies, frosted cakes and cupcakes, pudding made with whole milk or cream.

Candy

Everyday Choices

Each has less than 1 g of fat in a 100 calorie serving. Candied fruit, candy corn, fruit rolls, gummi bears, hard candies, gum, gumdrops, jelly beans, licorice, lollipops, marshmallows, hard mints, peppermint stick, maple syrup, chocolate syrup, jam, jelly, marmalade, marshmallow topping, taffy, Twizzlers.

Sometime Choices

Each has less than 3 g of fat in a 100 calorie serving. Caramels, candy cereals: Apple Cinnamon Cheerios, Apple Jacks (Kellogg's), Boo Berry (Gen Mills), Cap'n Crunch, Cocoa Krispies, Count Chocula (Gen Mills), Froot Loops, frosted cereals, Fruity Pebbles, Lucky Charms, Marshmallow Alpha-Bits, Reese's Puffs, Smacks (Kellogg's), Trix (Gen Mills).

Occasional Choices

All types of chocolate, including milk, semi-sweet, chocolate-covered nuts, chocolate candy bars, truffles.

Liquid Candy

Beverages are placed in this group if they carry 25 g of sugar per 100 calories.

Everyday Choices

NONE because it is just too easy to overconsume liquids. It is best if your child gets his candy from traditional sources. For example: soda is a liquid candy, and children can drink 150 calories very quickly, while a whole pack of

Life Savers, which carries 10 calories per piece, may take a day or more to finish.

Sometime Choices

Each has 25 g sugar in a serving, 100 calories, and is not a good source of nutrients. Capri Sun juice drink, Fruit Punch (most types), Hawaiian Punch fruit drinks, Kool-Aid fruit drinks, lemonade, limeade, sports drinks, sweetened ice tea, Twister juices, Sunbolt, Sunny Delight, Fruitopia, V8 Splash.

Occasional Choices

All soda and diet soda.

Others

Food in this group is used for flavor not nutrition. All seasonings listed here can be used freely, but sauces that are high in salt are not recommended for everyday use because they will teach your child to crave the taste of salt.

Everyday Choices

Flavoring extracts, fruit sauces, dried and fresh herbs, garlic powder and garlic juice, hot sauce, prepared horseradish. Salt used in cooking.

Sometime Choices

Tartar sauce, prepared mustard, tomato sauce, ketchup. BBQ sauce, soy sauce, steak sauce, seasoned salts.

Occasional Choices

Caramel sauce, chocolate sauce. Salt added at the table.

A NOTE ABOUT SALT

Discourage your children from getting in the habit of using salt at the table. You will notice small amounts can be used in cooking, but adding salt to cooked or prepared food should be an occasional choice. Keep salt off the table, and if your child does want to use it explain it is to be used occasionally, if at all.

Beverages

Count milk as a serving from the calcium group and all juice as a serving from the fruit group. All other noncaloric beverages in the Everyday choices can be enjoyed whenever thirsty.

Everyday Choices

Real fruit juice: apple juice, orange juice, grapefruit juice, pineapple juice; cow's milk, water, carbonated water (no sugar added) flavored and plain, herb tea.

Sometime Choices

Iced tea (sweetened), fruit blends, sports drinks.

Occasional Choices

All soda.

DIET SODA

Since the introduction of artificial sweeteners in the 1960s, the consumption of diet soda has gone out of sight, and yet we are more overweight than ever before. In theory, diet soda should help with weight loss, but it does not. The sweet taste in diet soda may actually increase appetite for real food, or perhaps it does not satisfy the body and overeating follows, or maybe it teaches an individual to crave sweet tastes. Whatever the reason, instead of being part of the solution, diet soda appears to be part of the problem. Do not teach your child that diet soda is an acceptable drink. Instead, teach her to drink the real thing and treat it like dessert or candy, as an Occasional not Everyday food.

THIRST QUENCHERS

Water is so important to our health it is actually considered a nutrient like vitamins and minerals. One food survey found that only two to three of the recommended eight cups of water we need daily is consumed as plain water. Milk, coffee, tea, soft drinks, and fruits and vegetables, which are 85 percent to 95 percent water, supply the rest. Such sources of fluid can be a good alternative to plain

water, but for many children they are a significant
source of empty calories and a cause of unwanted
weight gain. To keep your child well hydrated
offer him water throughout the day.

When he asks for something to drink, or you
are deciding on a beverage with a meal, consider
why you are serving it. Is it to quench thirst or
provide nutrition, or a combination of both? If
your child has consumed his recommended calcium choices in the form of yogurt or cheese,
additional milk is not needed at a meal, and water
might be a good choice. If your child has not
eaten the recommended servings of fruit, real
fruit juice can be a good beverage choice. What
you don't want to do is offer your child an unlimited supply of presweetened beverages, and this
includes sports drinks, fruit juice blends, and fruit
drinks. These are like drinking liquid candy and
too difficult for children to self-limit. Remember,
every 4 to 5 grams of sugar listed on the label is
the equivalent of one teaspoon of sugar. Many
sports drinks carry a sugar level almost equal to
soft drinks. Plain water, carbonated water, and
diluted lemonade or fruit juice are my recommended drink choices.

If your child is athletic, fluids are very important in regulating body temperature, metabolizing
food, and transporting nutrients and waste products. The sensation of thirst may not be a reliable
indicator of your child's need to drink. An active
child will lose fluid through sweat, breathing, and
urination—this is normal, and fluid can be replaced
by having something to drink. For most children

plain water will do, but I learned at one sports nutrition conference that children drink more when water is flavored. Offering diluted fruit juice or diluted sports drinks over plain water may improve consumption during athletic events. If your child lives in a hot climate or will be participating in very active workouts make sure she drinks enough the day before the event, and never allow a coach to tell your child to wear sauna suits or limit fluid during workouts. Clothing designed to prevent evaporation will prevent cooling and can be very dangerous for kids.

COMBINATION FOODS

Much of the food we eat is a combination of several foods, such as casseroles, stews, soup, and stir-fry. Combination recipes are a great way to serve several food groups in one simple but nutritious dish. Whenever there is a vegetable in the dish it counts as a serving from the vegetable group; if there is meat, cheese, fish, or beans in the dish, that counts as a serving from the protein group; if rice, noodles, or bread are in the mix then that counts as a serving from the grain/starch group—you get the idea!

Here are some examples of combination dishes and the food groups they contain:

Combination Dishes	**Food Groups**
1 cup (8 oz) tuna noodle casserole	2 bread/starch, 1 protein

Combination Dishes	Food Groups
1 cup macaroni and cheese*	2 grain/starch, 1 protein or 1 calcium
1 cup spaghetti with meatballs	1 grain/starch, 1 vegetable, 1 protein
1½ cup chicken stir-fry with rice	1 bread/starch, 1 vegetable, 1 protein
2-egg cheese and mushroom omelette	1 vegetable, 1 calcium, 1 protein
1¾ cup cereal with fruit and milk	2 bread/starch, 1 fruit, 1 calcium
2½" square of lasagne	1 grain/starch, 1 vegetable, 1 calcium, 1 protein
1 cheeseburger with lettuce and tomato	2 grain/starch, 1 vegetable, ½ calcium, 1 protein
1 baked potato with cheese and broccoli	2 vegetables, 1 calcium
1½ cup chef's salad	1 vegetable, 1 calcium, 1 protein
1 cup chili and crackers	1 grain/starch, 1 vegetable, 1 protein
⅙ of 12-inch cheese pizza	2 grain/starch, 1 protein

---

*Cheese can count as a calcium or protein source, but don't count it twice.

FROZEN, READY-TO-HEAT DINNERS

Frozen dinners have been around for decades and have advantages and disadvantages. They are quick and portion controlled, but most are low in calcium and fiber. Improve the nutrition quality of a frozen dinner by serving it with a glass of milk or yogurt and a slice of whole wheat bread, or cook some additional frozen vegetables or brown rice to boost the fiber. Dinners with fewer than 300 calories are too low in calories and should be served with the above suggestions to prevent overeating later on. Dinners designed specifically for kids are not as bad as you might expect—serve them occasionally. Most contain around 500 calories, 4 to 6 g of fiber, and a fat intake that ranges between 5 to 19 g. Calcium is usually low, as are vitamins A and C, but this can be improved by serving it with a glass of milk and offering some extra fruit if still hungry.

One way to evaluate a frozen or any ready-to-eat dinner is to compare the nutrition label to what a child needs in a day. At each meal a child should eat approximately one-third of what he needs for a day. See the box on how to assess fast-food meals and frozen dinners, on page 145. In general, frozen dinners are much better than the prepackaged, refrigerated boxed lunches sold in the deli cases—just compare the labels. What I don't like about these meals is that they do not support communal eating, something kids need to learn and experience often.

Everyday Choices

Any combination made from the Everyday choices in any of the food groups.

Sometime Choices

Any combination dish that contains more than 3 ounces of full-fat cheese per serving; frozen TV dinners for kids; low-fat frozen meals.

Occasional Choices

Fried combination foods, frozen chicken pot pie, recipes made from one or more foods from the Occasional choice in any food group. Meals that contain more than one-third of a child's need for sodium or fat or sugar, respectively, that is, approximately 22 g of fat, 800 mg sodium, 15 g of sugar. The following foods are listed as Occasional choices because of their high sodium content: canned stew, canned macaroni, canned hash, cream or cheese soup.

EATING AWAY FROM HOME

One source states that 46 percent of our food money goes to eating food away from home. The most popular food children order when out are french fries and soda. Most parents will order what they know their kids will eat—pizza, fries, burgers, and not spend money on a salad or side of vegetables that may go uneaten. If you and your family eat out once per week, for a pizza or a burger, have your child order what he wants but count the fried foods in the once-per-week recommendation and the servings of full-fat cheese as part of the twice-per-week suggestion. At other meals and snacks, make up for any fruit or vegetable you may have missed. If you eat meals away from home more than once per week you must evaluate what you are ordering and make sure it fits in with your child's need for nutrition. Ask your child to order a regular burger not a large, or a roast beef sandwich, which is leaner than most burgers. Order a baked potato instead of fries and a skim milk instead of a shake or soda. Order a salad (share it if you have to) and try pizza with vegetables on top. If your child has a soda, switch to water after it is finished and *DON'T SUPERSIZE ANYTHING*, no matter how good the price.

WATCH YOUR PORTIONS

When researchers at Pennsylvania State University fed preschoolers, ages three and five, portions of macaroni and cheese they found that the older children, but not the younger ones, ate more when given larger servings. This study suggests that by the end of the preschool years, the amount of food offered a child will influence how much food he eats, making it important to serve appropriate size portions, which is why you don't want to "supersize" an order of fries or a soft drink or make a child clean his plate. Instead, parents need to be aware of what portions of each food group young children actually require.

At Chinese restaurants order plain rice and steamed vegetables with meals and eat as much of these as the main dish or appetizers you order. Fried foods are abundant in Chinese restaurants—anything called "breaded" or "crispy" is deep fried. Share main dishes and take half home.

The next time you go out to eat, if the table is loaded with fried food or high-fat cheese foods talk to your kids about what they ordered. Use the opportunity to point out the absence of fruit, vegetables, and the addition of fats and maybe empty calories in the form of soda. Don't ruin the fun of the meal but point out that it is hard to get at restaurants the food needed for good health. Such a conversation is part of being thoughtful, mindful eaters.

Most schools participate in the U.S. government's school lunch program. Despite its past reputation, the school lunch program is trying to serve more healthful meals. To be successful they need your help. An excellent nutrition program available to all schools for the asking is the U.S. Department of Agriculture's Team Nutrition Program. Be aware of what your school is providing in school vending machines. Some school systems are contracting with beverage companies to sell a minimum amount of soda or fruit drinks, and in turn the soda company will provide the school with funds for education. The problem with this marriage is that it is selling our children's health down the drain. Soda is replacing other essential food groups. This may seem like a harmless way to raise money but it isn't. It tells children that their health is not important to the community. Is this the message we want to send to our children? Is this the best we can do? No, it isn't. Change the drinks to real fruit juice, and real fruit. Send a message to your kids that health is as important as money.

HOW TO EVALUATE YOUR CHILD'S FAVORITE FRANCHISE MEAL, READY-TO-EAT, OR FROZEN DINNER

All fast-food restaurants have nutrition information available for the asking (see Resources for Web site information), and all prepared meals carry a nutrition label. Ask your child to pick his favorite franchise meal or prepared meal sold at the supermarket. Using the nutrition information provided by the franchise or food company calculate the total calories, fat, sodium, and fiber provided in a meal and compare it to what your child needs. Also determine which food groups are represented. For example, a six-year-old boy may require about 1,800 calories, 66 g fat, and 11 g fiber daily and doesn't need more than 2,400 mg sodium or 40 g of added sugar in a day. One-third of this should theoretically be eaten at each meal, meaning a meal should carry about 600 calories, 22 g fat, and 4 g fiber and not more than 800 mg sodium and 15 g sugar. A meal should also include one-third of all the food groups—at least one fruit, one vegetable, two grains, one-third of a child's daily calcium requirement, and a serving of protein if it is a main meal. Below is a sample meal. How does it meet our six-year-old's needs?

FOOD	FAT (G)	CAL	SODIUM	FIBER	SUGAR
Hamburger	12	275	474	3	—
Reg. french fries	12	235	124	2.4	—

Food	Fat (g)	Cal	Sodium	Fiber	Sugar
12-oz soda	0	151	35	—	40
low-fat cone	1	105	92	0.1	*
Total	25	766	725	5.5	40+
⅓ recommended fat and calories	22	600	800	4	15

*Not available

Food groups represented: protein and grain/starch. Food groups missing: fruit, vegetable, calcium (the cone does not carry enough calcium to make it count as a serving from the calcium group).

How do you think this meal rates? The absence of fruits, vegetables, and whole grains is the worst part of the meal. It isn't too high in total fat or calories because the choices were regular, not super size. Your child can certainly handle a meal like this once in a while. It is your responsibility to make sure meals at home make up for the fruits, vegetables, and Real food your child missed. If you eat out once a week or rely on prepackaged or frozen meals only once per week but eat the rest of your meals during scheduled mealtimes at home with planned menus that are low in fat, then your overall diet over seven days will be okay.

HOW LONG BEFORE I SEE AN EFFECT?

Every child is unique, and the immediate effect may be different from what you expect. For example, once you clarify that nutrition is your guide to food choices, and you implement a regular eating routine and the One-Bite Rule, you may find food arguments and food struggles disappear. You will also feel less anxious about your child's weight because you are reacting and responding to the issue in a positive way.

It is impossible to predict bodily changes. If you are implementing a thought-out plan of eating and exercise you will be directing your child to eat and live in a way that will help him attain his natural and healthy weight. When you do see a change in your child, use words such as *healthy*, *strong*, or *fit* to describe how he looks. Stay away from words like *skinny* or comments such as "I knew you wouldn't always be fat." Keep the focus on health and not on appearance. You have no control over your child's weight and neither does she. All you can control is the food that is available in the home and the environment where it is consumed.

DO'S AND DON'TS THAT WILL MAKE THE REAL FOOD DIET EASIER AND HEALTHFUL

Do's

Do strive to eat a "Balanced Diet" over a seven-day period. No single day matters, it is the cumulative effect of what we eat that counts.

Do make thoughtful decisions about what you buy to drink.

Do make compromises about dessert or food you argue about.

(For example, if your child loves chicken pot pie but it is high in fat, find a way to serve it occasionally, such as once per week or on a day that your child is particularly active. If your child says he is "dying" to try a new novelty food, let him. When my kids were younger they wanted to try every new food they saw advertised, from blue gelatin to holiday creme–filled snack cakes. I would let them try them once. We'd have it for a snack or dessert and look at the nutrition label to count the sugar and to see if it carried fiber, calcium, or other redeeming nutrients—it almost never did. When it was gone, that was it. I didn't buy it again, and they didn't feel like they were missing anything. The goal is for your child and you to be thoughtful about what is eaten, not to eliminate favorite foods.)

Do serve five or more fruits and vegetables daily.

Do talk about healthful eating guidelines before putting them into effect at the table.

Do serve three whole grain foods daily to adults and teens and one or more servings to young children.

Do serve fish at least once per week.

Do serve beans as a main dish at least once per week.

Do eat a meatless meal once per week.

Do eat or serve nuts once per week. These are a good source of hard-to-get nutrients.

Do consume the recommended serving from the calcium group.

Do drink or serve 1 percent or skim milk (after age two).

Do drink or serve water or diluted fruit juice to quench thirst.

Don'ts

Don't eat full-fat cheese more than twice per week.

Don't eat fried food more than once per week (this includes chips).

Don't eat pizza more than once per week.

Don't skip meals.

Don't eat after supper.

Don't eat more than one snack food carrying 500 mg of sodium per serving, per day.

Don't eat the skin on poultry.

Don't drink fruit drinks, "ade" (lemonade, limeade), or "punch" as a thirst quencher.

Don't shop without a list.

Don't keep track of whose eating what at the table—it could turn your table into a battleground.

The Real Food Diet is based on good nutrition. It is not a diet that encourages hunger or deprivation. Instead it promotes the eating of good, simple food, and it requires that parents and children be thoughtful and mindful about what they eat. Children and families who plan meals based on the Everyday, Sometime, and Occasional choices think about what they eat and how they eat. By regularly eating together they can reach their natural weights and enjoy good health physically and emotionally. Let your child eat what he needs from these food groups and he will be on a diet of customary and usual foods that will lead him toward his natural weight.

7

≡

Putting It All Together: Exercise, Food, Family

So much of the way we believe is because of how we've been brought up. I think that if parents can be taught that it's important for them to start kids with good eating habits, then they'll have big rewards for the kids once they start to eat by themselves.

—TENTH-GRADE BOY

One definition of family is "those who eat together."

—MARGARET VISSER, *JOURNAL OF GASTRONOMY*

Although most families break bread together regularly, there are still a large number who cannot find the time for family meals.

—TALKING WITH TEENS: THE YMCA PARENT AND TEEN SURVEY

Good nutrition is not enough in a family where weight has become an issue. Inclusion of regular activity and an understanding of the family's attitude toward food is of equal importance. In this chapter you will develop family goals that will support your efforts to eat healthier, exercise more, and create a plan of action to fulfill these goals.

In this chapter there are four exercises to complete with as many family members as you can involve (preferably everyone). Your child does not live in isolation, he lives in a family. How the family speaks about food, weight, and diets, and the value the family places on food and health will have as powerful an effect on your child as the food he eats. For this reason goals are stated as family goals, not individual goals.

Exercise One: The Family Food Record

Have each family member keep a one-day food record. The point of this exercise is to become familiar with the food groups each member needs, to identify the food groups that are being over- or underconsumed, and most of all start the conversation that nutrition and food are important in your home.

Young children usually enjoy this exercise, older kids may say it is annoying, but try to get everyone involved. Older teens can be asked to help younger siblings and to set an example. It is best if both parents are involved too. If one parent does not participate it will send the message loud and clear that something in this activity is not valued. If your children are not yet school-age you can do the writing for them, but keep track of your own food intake too.

Make copies of the one-day food record on page 153 for each family member, or use a piece of lined paper and copy the questions. Have each family member fill in the food groups they need daily, using the chart next to the food diary.

Starting at breakfast, keep track of what is eaten for the day, including all solid and liquid foods and portion sizes. Look at the food groups in chapter 6 if you are unsure where a food belongs or how big a portion is. A 12-ounce bottle of juice counts as at least two fruits not one. A 12-ounce prime rib is equal to four protein choices. Do not count foods more than once. For example, don't count cheese in the Calcium group and the Protein group. Do record your intake of fat/oil and snack/sweet/other foods. As you do this exercise you will find some groups over-represented while others are underrepresented. Adults are often low in the fruit and calcium groups, kids are often low in the vegetable group and sometimes high in the calcium group. Most Americans young and old eat enough from the protein group, and intake from the fat/oil and snack/sweet/other groups can vary widely.

Don't be too surprised if this exercise does not go smoothly. It is not uncommon for one family member to think this is a worthwhile exercise while others are not as enthusiastic. Don't get discouraged. Though the stated goal of this activity is to assess how everybody in the family does at obtaining the food groups they need, the real goal is to start the conversation that wholesome food and good nutrition are something your family is going to strive for. It will also make each family member aware of the number of food groups they need to eat every day to maintain their best health and make them think about what they put into their mouths. The conversation you want to start is that nutrition is important for every family member, no matter what his or her size or age.

Once the food record is complete have everyone write down the food groups that are over- or underrepresented in their food record. The exercise is complete when the assessment questions are answered at the bottom of the food record page.

Review Exercise One

Based on the food records your family kept, list the food groups that need to be increased in the family diet and those that need to be decreased. Make this list as long as you need to. What goals in regard to food groups do you need to set? List as many goals as you need but pick the five you think are most important. List your family's food goals below. Every family member should contribute at least one food goal.

EXERCISE ONE: ONE-DAY FOOD RECORD

HOW MANY SERVINGS DO YOU NEED EACH DAY?

	Women, Some Older Adults, Children Ages 4–6*	Children, Teen Girls, Active Women, Most Men	Teen Boys, Active Men
Grain/Starch	6	9	11
Vegetable	3	4	5
Fruit	2	3	4
Calcium	2–3**	2–3**	2–3**
Protein	2 (for a total of 5 ounces)	2 (for a total of 6 ounces)	2 (for a total of 7 ounces)
Fat/Oil	3–6	3–6	3–6

---

*Children under age 4 can follow the same food guidelines, but make portions smaller, about two-thirds of a regular portion.

**Women who are pregnant or breast-feeding, teenagers, and young adults to age 24 need 3 servings.

Food Diary

TIME	FOOD	AMOUNT
Breakfast		
Morning snack		
Lunch		
Afternoon snack		
Dinner		
Evening snack		

Number of Food Group Servings You Need Every Day		**Number Eaten**
Grain/Starch	___	___
Vegetable	___	___
Fruit	___	___
Calcium	___	___
Protein	___	___

What food groups are low or missing?_____

_____

What food groups are overrepresented? _____

_____

How many servings from the Snack/Sweet/Other category? _____

Sample Family Food Goals

Our family's food goals include:

Consuming the recommended servings from all the food groups.

Snacking from the everyday choices in the grain/starch group when hungry.

Limiting food choices from the snack/sweet/other group to twice per day.

Limiting food from the calcium group to no more than three per day.

Eating only the recommended amount from the protein group.

Shopping once per week, buying enough fresh or frozen vegetables to last the week.

Your Family's Food Goals

Our Family's Food Goals include:

_____

_____

_____

WRITING SUCCESSFUL GOALS

Goals should be: believable, achievable, measurable, and stated positively. After stating a goal ask yourself:

Do I believe in this goal?

Is it realistic to expect I can achieve this goal?

Can I measure this goal?

Is this goal stated in the positive? Such as "I will
eat fruit when I need a snack" instead of "I
won't eat cake or candy when I'm hungry."

EXERCISE TWO: THE FAMILY ACTIVITY LEVEL

Over the past seven days, how many days have you and
each family member been physically active and for how
long? On a separate piece of paper have each family
member write the days of the week, ending with today's
day. Have each family member write any activity they
were involved in this week next to the day of the week it
occurred and write the duration of the activity. Help one
another remember exercise such as recess, walks, basketball, and so on. Anything that can cause a little perspira-
tion can be defined as activity—walking, running, active
play, organized sports, active recess, dancing, jumping,
raking, heavy gardening, or cleaning. Read more about
your need for exercise and what counts as exercise in
chapter 4. Example for fifth-grade girl:

Wednesday	15-minute recess at school—twice
Thursday	walk the puppy 5 minutes, open gym before school 18 minutes
Friday	15-minute recess at school—twice, ride bike to friend's house 10 minutes
Saturday	30-minute walk with Mom
Sunday	nothing
Monday	15-minute recess at school twice, bas-ketball 1½ hours
Tuesday	Recess at school 15 minutes once

Evaluate Activity

If you meet the following activity recommendations for your age, then rate your activity as good; if it is only half of what you require, rate yourself fair; and if you were not active at all, rate your activity level as poor. You want to strive for a good rating.

Young children (elementary age and younger): provide young children with the opportunity to be active at least four to five times a week.

Adolescents: be active on most days and engage in three or more exercise sessions per week that last twenty minutes or more.

Adults: three to five exercise sessions per week, strength training two to three times per week.

What is the overall activity level of your family? Rate it as good, fair, or poor.

Review Exercise 2

Based on the results of exercise 2 what goals for physical activity does your family need to incorporate to put all family members at a good level of activity? Come up with at least five goals and have each family member contribute at least one goal.

Sample Family Exercise Goals

We will strive to be an active family: we will use the stairs at work and ride our bikes to school when the weather is good.

We will take turns walking the dog fifteen minutes every day.

Suzie will go to open gym each Thursday.

Peter will play basketball at least three times during the
    week.

We will take a family bike ride every weekend.

    Remember, when setting goals children are motivated
100 percent by fun!!

Your Family's Exercise Goals

Our Family's Exercise Goals include:

_____

_____

_____

_____

_____

EXERCISE THREE: THE FAMILY FOOD STYLE QUIZ

The purpose of this exercise is to identify family food
habits that may slow your progress or contribute to poor
nutrition. Once again complete this with as many family
members as you can, leaving out the babies of course. Single parents of young children can do this solo. You must
answer yes or no, not maybe or sometimes. Be prepared
for jokes, silliness, and maybe even an uncooperative
spirit. Children can distract with humor or the "I forgots."
Let them know this is important. This will send the message to the family and set in motion the process of change
in the family. As much as possible try to make this fun.
You are not striving for perfection, you are starting a conversation that will lead to changes in your family's food

style and habits. Simply by taking the time to do this activity the conversation has begun, and this in itself sends a very positive message about the value you place on family, food, and nutrition.

Answer yes or no to the following questions. Does your family:

1. Have a regularly scheduled mealtime?

2. Eat meals together that last fifteen minutes or more?

3. Avoid making family members "clean their plate"?

4. Avoid television during meals?

5. Have a thought-out list of appropriate snacks to eat between meals?

6. Eat only at a designated area (kitchen, dining room)?

7. Have ways to celebrate accomplishments other than with food?

8. Have time to plan and shop for food?

9. Snack only when hungry and not to ease boredom or soothe emotions?

10. Avoid late night snacking?

11. Avoid using food as a means of punishment?

12. Know how to read a food label?

13. Avoid phrases such as: "that will make you fat," "I need to go on a diet," "we are a fat family," "everything that tastes good is bad for you"?

14. Avoid prohibiting favorite food because it is thought to be fattening?

15. Avoid making any family member eat when not hungry because "it is good for you"?

16. Have a routine of regular physical exercise?

17. Keep the scale in an out-of-the-way location?

18. Eat a menu of naturally low-fat foods and not heavily processed diet foods?

19. Plan meals together?

20. Eat five fruits and vegetables each day?

21. Treat soda as if it were liquid candy?

22. Know how to cook?

23. Know what each member needs to eat to have a "balanced diet"?

How to Use Your Responses

Each no answer is intended to identify an area that will not support a goal of good nutrition and healthful eating. A no answer may identify a family food style practice that is causing or assisting a weight problem. Read below the reasons your no response may indicate a trouble spot and read the suggested alternate response to try to address the issue.

1. Regular Meals

A regular meal schedule can help your child feel secure. Young children thrive on routines, and it will help a child to better self-regulate food intake. A regular meal schedule can help control in-between-meal snacking and help prevent a child from eating right before a meal. When there is no regular meal schedule it is harder to plan to meet nutrition needs and can lead to overeating snacks. Turn to page 98 for a suggested meal schedule that the entire family can use.

2. Eating Together for Fifteen Minutes or More

Families tend to eat better and include more variety when they eat together. Eating together promotes social skills, and one study says conversation at meals leads to better word comprehension and reading skills. It takes about fifteen minutes before any group (including families) can settle in and start a conversation, and it also takes that long to reach satiety. Rushed meals can promote excessive calorie intake because they do not allow for a child's natural satiety control to kick in. Overweight children have been observed to eat significantly faster than children of normal weight.

If your family is consistently eating a hot dog on the way to a game or a slice of pizza at the snack shack or a fast-food meal on the way to a lesson you are telling your children that eating together and proper nutrition are not important when you are busy. Is this the message you want to send? If not, plan ahead. See Eating on the Run on page 234 in chapter 8. In terms of family cohesiveness supper does not have to be your family mealtime; lots of households count on breakfast as the time to eat together. Just make sure there is enough time allowed so it's not too hectic. Set the table the night before, be packed for school, that kind of thing. Be prepared for the routine activities in your schedule, and plan ahead of time.

3. Clean Your Plate

Telling a child to clean his plate when he is full is teaching him to overeat. If there is too much food on the plate, or too much milk in the glass, tell your child to pour less or serve himself less. If you are doing the serving, cut back and serve seconds on request. Healthy children will eat what they need. You only need to provide them with the food and a place free of distractions. Telling a child to clean his plate is not the same as telling him to try his vegetables. The One-Bite rule is recommended because it encourages variety and trying new things. Since the rule also says it is safe to leave an unacceptable food on the dish, it does not override the child's ability to distinguish fullness.

4. Television

There is a link between excessive television watching and being overweight. In a Johns Hopkins University survey, researchers found that a fourth of all children in the United States watch more than four hours of TV per day, and these children were fatter than children who watched fewer than two hours per day. In a Harvard School of Public Health study there was a strong relationship between being overweight and hours of television watched. In this group of 746, more than 60 percent of the incidence of overweight in ten- to fifteen-year-olds was linked to excessive television watching.

TV watching is sedentary, and kids often eat high-fat, high-calorie snack foods while watching TV. In a TV programming survey, 21.1 commercials were counted during an hour of children's programming. Food advertisements counted for half of these ads, and 90 percent of the ads advertised foods high in fat, sugar, and salt. Your children will rarely see an ad for wholesome foods such as fruits, vegetables, and low-sugar cereals. If watching television is always accompanied by snacking, then your child can eat hundreds, perhaps a thousand extra calories without being hungry. One of the reasons Americans have gained so much weight is because they eat thoughtlessly while they watch TV. Most children who are overweight watch more than two hours of TV per day. To blunt the effect of the media parents need to watch TV with their kids and point out the absence of balanced advertising. Unfortunately 46 percent of U.S. adults believe their neighborhoods are unsafe, and TV is seen as a safe after-school activity that is often encouraged by working parents. Organized activities before and after school, such as open gyms, are needed in every community.

Kids who watch TV while eating miss out on the intellectual and creative rapport they can obtain from family members. In the book *How Good Parents Raise Great Kids* the author identifies many characteristics that superior students share. One of them includes that they watched TV one-third of the national average of seven hours per day. Turn off the TV during meals, limit the hours it is on, and find an activity that is more active. Your child will probably do better in school and lose weight simultaneously.

5. Appropriate Snacks

You can avoid food battles and poor snack choices if you are proactive in this area. Talk to your children about what they would like to eat between meals. Together come up with a list that combines their need for nutrition and their desire for fun foods. See the list of snacks on page 101. Some families designate a snack shelf that is stocked with foods kids can eat between meals anytime, such as individual containers of fruit, ready-to-eat cereal, whole wheat crackers.

6. Eating in One Spot

Eating in one, maybe two areas such as the kitchen and the dining room is an effective way to promote conscious eating and awareness of what is being consumed. If a child takes a whole box of graham crackers to his room while he watches TV he is more apt to overeat because he is eating thoughtlessly. But ask him to eat only at the kitchen table and he will have more success at correctly self-regulating based on hunger.

7. Celebrating Acomplishments

Some celebrations, such as birthday parties, go hand in hand with food. But always rewarding good grades or a clean room with food is not recommended because such an association can create a lifelong habit of self-rewarding with food. Try nonfood celebrations such as reading a book together, going for a walk, planning a swimming or roller-skating date.

8. Planning and Shopping

Eating better starts with a shopping list. If you consistently: grab food on the run, shop more than once per week, or come home from the market with foods you never intended to buy, then you absolutely need to make a list before you head to the store. A list will help you cut down on impulse buying and will make you plan for the fruits, vegetables, and snacks you need to have in your home and to promote good nutrition. See the sample grocery list in chapter 8 and the advice on getting kids to help and cooperate while shopping. Involving other family members in creating the shopping list will promote conscious choice of healthy foods.

9. Snacking

Snacking to ease boredom or to change a mood is eating out of emotional hunger. The child who uses food to release tension or anxiety can create a lifelong use of food to ease these emotions. It is important to redirect your child to a more positive response to these emotional triggers. If you suspect your child is eating emotionally ask her if she is really hungry. If she is, then she should eat from a wholesome list of snacks. If she is not truly hungry try an alternate activity to ease emotional tension. Physical activity is a terrific tension buster; ask her to kick a soccer ball or shoot some hoops, or take a walk together. Encourage hobbies: find a puzzle book or building blocks or a paint-by-number set to redirect the energy. Most of all, try to get your child to see the difference between eating when hungry and eating when bored. You don't have to tell her what to do, just ask her to think about whether she really needs to eat. Put the responsibility about food where it belongs, with her.

10. Late-Night Snacking

Late-night eating is a major issue in overweight adults. It is a very hard habit to break, so try to prevent your young child from forming this habit. Encourage children under age twelve to consider supper as the last eating event of the day. If your child is hungry after dinner or if he ate very early, provide him with only simple food choices such as toast, fruit, a graham cracker. Eating ice cream, pudding, even diet foods all create the desire for food at night and late-night eating has the potential to be a very serious source of excessive calories now and later in adulthood.

11. Food as Punishment

Using food to punish can make a child feel anxious, and it can give the food being withheld special status. You also teach your child that food can be a source of control, and you may teach him to refuse food as a means to punish you. If there is a need to discipline your child, make sure the punishment fits the crime. If your child was supposed to clean his room and didn't, I'd recommend withholding television and asking him to clean his room plus an additional room or closet. Withholding food is almost always an inappropriate response to wrongdoing.

12. Food Labels

Learning to read food labels can be a lot of fun. Ask your kids to compare the nutrition value of a variety of foods. Cereal boxes are a very effective way to learn how to read a label because they can vary so widely in nutrition content. Compare the amount of fiber, protein, vitamins, percentage of calcium, sodium, and sugar. Don't focus just on calories because you may teach that a no-calorie food, such as a diet drink, is good when actually it contains no nutrition at all.

13. Family Speak

The words you use to describe your family and their eating habits will be prophetic. Your child listens to everything you say and absorbs it like a sponge, so make sure the words you say are actually sending the message you want. Use phrases like "Johnny is learning to try new foods," or "Jenny is doing so well at learning to cook," or "the whole family is working on getting the exercise we need and I feel stronger for it." These are examples of positive statements that will be helpful in meeting your family food goals. Comments such as "our family has always been fat" or "as soon as I start to eat healthily I get sick" are statements that will slow or prevent your family's progress toward better health.

14. Limiting Favorite Foods

Every food can be fattening. If a family member has a food jag and loves cheese or cake or hot dogs or peanut butter or canned spaghetti don't forbid them but put them in their proper place. Allow the peanut butter sandwich, but keep it to one serving and serve other foods to round out the menu. If a child only wants macaroni and cheese offer a portion but also include other foods and ask him to eat them. The real issue is that no one food provides a growing child with the nutrition he needs, and if a child wants one particular food ask him to try other foods too. Don't make it a good or bad issue; turn it into a health issue. Read about Young Kids, Food, Taste, and Development on page 97.

15. Eat, It's Good for You

Telling a child they must eat tells them that you know better than they do, how hungry your child really is, but you can't possibly know this with any real accuracy. If there is a structure in place for scheduled meals that include a variety of food, kids will eat what they need and get the nutrition they need. Do encourage the One-Bite Rule but don't force anybody to eat. You set the menu of healthy food, they choose from the food you offer.

16. Exercise

Each family member over age twelve should exercise regularly. Younger children need to be active too, but this can take the form of active play and doesn't need to be scheduled, as it usually does for older kids. Mom and Dad need their exercise too. If you're not sure what counts as exercise or how much a family member requires reread chapter 3.

17. The Scale

Try not to teach your children that the scale is important. Keep the scale in an inconvenient location or get rid of it altogether. If your family is active and eating well you will see the difference in the mirror and feel it in your clothes. Your child will be weighed when he goes to the doctor and your doctor can keep track of this information. The family focus should be on food and activity not the scale. This program is about feeling good and healthy not achieving a certain number.

18. Naturally Low-Fat, Minimally Processed Foods

The food you bring into your kitchen, and eat when away from home, will dictate your health and body weight. Select naturally low-fat food (this includes all the Everyday choices listed in chapter 6), aim for a diet that is minimally processed—not high in sodium or sugar or void of fiber. Avoid diet foods. Diet foods do not help people lose weight. Read about diet soda on page 137.

19. Plan Meals

Ask your family what they want to eat—fruits and vegetables, cereals and snacks. Put the responsibility for

healthy eating on them. This will promote better acceptance and take some of the burden off of you as well as
help the rest of the family become conscious eaters.

20. Five a Day

Quite simply, to be as healthy as you can, to prevent obesity, heart disease, and cancer everyone in the family has
to eat fruits and vegetables. If you have trouble getting
your child to eat vegetables then offer four fruits and one
vegetable and keep trying to get as much variety as possible. This five-a-day advice goes for Mom, Dad, and older
siblings too.

21. Soda Is Candy

Soda is the fastest growing food group in the U.S. diet.
There is nothing wrong with a can of soda, just as there is
nothing wrong with a candy bar. But you wouldn't serve
candy instead of breakfast and you shouldn't serve soda
instead of milk or juice. Keep soda in its place. It is a fun
snack, and like having ice cream or a candy bar it should
not be an everyday thing in anyone's menu, and that
includes diet soda too. Read about diet soda on page 137.

22. Get Cooking

Learning to cook will give a child a sense of accomplishment, and when the child is older it can really be a source
of help to parents. Cooking can start as a hobby and later
become a vocation. It can teach a child what goes into a
recipe, which will help them understand why a chocolate
cake made with expensive and rich ingredients is consid-

ered special or why a Danish pastry made flaky by layers of butter is best eaten only on special occasions. On page 197 read what your child should learn to cook by the time he reaches age eighteen.

23. Balanced Diet

If you don't know where you want to go, you can't get there. By the time your child enters kindergarten or first grade she should have a basic knowledge of the food she needs to eat every day to maintain health. Use the recommended food servings in the Food Guide Pyramid and the results of Exercise One to teach about nutrition and food needs. Your child will learn very little in the way of meaningful information about food from her teachers or her doctor. If she doesn't learn about food from you she will learn about it from advertisers. Who do you want teaching her about food?

Review Exercise Three

A no response in the Family Food Style Quiz identifies an area that may be the cause of inappropriate eating in your family. Based on the quiz and the explanation that followed it, list all the areas identified by the Family Food Style Quiz that you feel should be altered in your family. Be as specific as possible, and the list can be as long as you need it to be.

Sample List of Issues

We make fun of overeating and being fat.
We don't speak positively about each family member.

We need a list of healthy and favorite between-meal snacks.

We need to eat together as a family more often.

We watch TV, read the newspaper, and talk on the phone during mealtimes.

We eat snacks after supper.

We don't know how to cook.

We don't allow dessert if the plate isn't "cleaned."

Your Family's Food Style Issues

_____

_____

_____

_____

_____

Based on your Family Food Style Issues listed above, develop a goal or goals that will correct or control these issues.

Sample Family Food Style Goals

We will speak positively about eating healthy.

We will allow each family member to choose his own portions but everybody will practice the One-Bite Rule.

We will eat together three times a week for dinner and at every breakfast.

We will only eat fruit after supper.

We will learn how to cook three new vegetables.

Your Family's Food Style Goals

_____

_____

_____

_____

_____

CHILDREN LOSE WEIGHT MORE EFFECTIVELY WHEN FAMILY THERAPY IS PART OF THE TREATMENT

In a study of obese six- to twelve-year-old children Dr. Epstein, of the University of Pittsburgh, found that when parents were involved children were more successful at losing weight. Seventy-six children and their parents were randomly assigned to one of three groups. Each group was assigned a similar diet and exercise program, and participated in behavior management training. In group one, parent and child worked together; in group two, only the child's behavior and weight loss were reinforced; and in group three, only attendance was reinforced. The researchers followed the families over a ten-year period. Children in group number one, the child-parent group, showed significantly greater decrease in percent overweight after five and ten years at follow-up over group three, and children in group two showed an increase in percent overweight. The researchers conclude that children will be more successful with weight loss when parents are involved. Based on this research, when treatment is started early, between ages six and twelve, its positive effects can persist into young adulthood.

In other research, this time in Sweden, 1,774 children ages ten to eleven were enrolled in a study designed to evaluate the effect family therapy can have on childhood obesity. The children were divided into two groups, and each group received similar treatment including diet counseling and a medical checkup. The only difference between the groups was that in one group the whole family participated in family therapy. In the group receiving family therapy the therapists reinforced the resources of the family, with the goal of creating an optimal emotional climate for helping the obese child. Sessions were scheduled at two- to three-month intervals, which allowed the families time to change. At follow-up—when children were fourteen years old—the children in the family therapy group had a significantly lower BMI than the other treatment group and a control group. In this case the addition of family therapy created a positive emotional environment for the child that was effective in weight control.

In *Obesity Evaluation and Treatment and Expert Committee Recommendation* the authors conclude that "parenting skills are the foundation for successful intervention that puts in place gradual, targeted increases in activity and targeted reductions in high-fat, high-calorie foods."

EXERCISE 4: DEVELOP A PLAN OF ACTION

Don't rush into this. Take your time and be thoughtful and not overly rigid. Using the information from the three previous exercises, identify the goals you feel are most important to your family. Be specific. Start with only five, and you may want to choose those you believe will be easy and where you can find the most success. It is better to start small and work up than to start big and give up. You will use leftover goals later on.

The plan of action should be written as actions you need to take today to meet your goals for food, exercise and family.

Sample Family Plan of Action

We will develop a family meal schedule and use this and the Everyday choices in the food groups to create a food shopping list.

We will write on the calendar the days we can walk or be active in a sport.

We will write a list of healthy snacks and post it on the refrigerator.

We will eat three fruits and vegetables every day.

We will speak positively about eating healthy food and about one another's appearance.

Notice I have used the pronoun *we* in my example. It would be terrific if the entire family took part in these goals and the family plan of action. In reality, depending on age and the interest level of other family members, there may only be one person—you—who will be writing out the plan of action. That is okay, as long as you are the person who organizes the family food schedule. You will need to communicate your new food goals and plan of action to everybody it effects. I find if a family member has participated in each exercise they will be invested in the end result. If there has been no initial participation, then implementing change can be more difficult. Don't get discouraged. If you institute a needed meal schedule, or a rule about eating fruits and vegetables, or develop a list of appropriate snacks, you have started the family on an improved diet, and just these three changes can improve your child's health tremendously.

When you start to use the food groups to select your Everyday foods you will automatically be changing the family's diet of customary and usual foods to those that will help everyone reach and maintain their natural weight and get the nutrition they need.

Your Family's Plan of Action

_____

_____

_____

_____

_____

Evaluate your plan of action. Does this plan address the need for scheduled meals, planned snacks, thoughtful shopping? Does the plan put the emphasis on healthy living over weight loss alone? Is the need for regular activity included? Does the plan feel manageable to you? Do you feel good about it? Does the family and your child feel good about it? If you answer yes to these questions start your plan of action today.

CAN THERE BE AN INDIVIDUAL PLAN OF ACTION?

Yes. Adolescents and teens, even adults can develop and monitor their own personal goals and their own plan of action. But it should parallel family goals, and it must be realistic and measurable in order to be successful.

DOES EVERYBODY NEED TO DO THIS?

Even if there is only one child in the family who is over-weight, every member of the family can benefit from better nutrition. Even "skinny" kids may not be well nourished. Remember the *Pediatrics* report cited earlier that found only 1 percent of young people surveyed ate the recommended servings of the food groups and a full 16 percent did not meet the recommendation for any of the food servings.

While being overweight is obvious, being poorly nourished is less so. Seven of the top killers in the United States, which include heart disease, lung cancer, diabetes, colo-rectal cancer, breast cancer, prostrate cancer, and osteoporosis, are not likely to affect your children until they reach adulthood, but the risk factors for these killers can start in childhood, and proper diet is a way to prevent them. The diet that can treat obesity is the same diet that will prevent disease. Even the normal or underweight child is susceptible to becoming overweight when he reaches adulthood. One-third of American adults are now overweight, and your normal weight child can fall into this statistic as he ages if he is not making intelligent food choices. Besides the health benefits good food can provide, a good diet is part of responsible parenting. In a popular book: *Ask the Children: What American Children Think About Working Parents* by Ellen Galinsky, the author interviewed over one thousand children about their lives. Galinsky writes that regular activities such as eating meals together, taking walks, or discussing homework have a positive effect on how children view their parents and how the child herself develops. One child said, "If you are leading by example, if you are following what you preach, then your kids will turn out pretty good."

We want to lead by example, and food provides parents with an excellent opportunity. The environment parents create around food can promote health, personal responsibility, and strengthen the family. This environment involves more than good nutrition and food selection; it is the whole attitude and the value food takes within a family. Your efforts at improving the family's health through better diet and more exercise may not always go smoothly or as planned, but the effort is worthwhile and is an essential part of a total plan to help your child reach his natural weight.

LIVE YOUR PLAN OF ACTION

Incorporate your plan of action into your routine for one month. Spend a few minutes each week planning meals and scheduling exercise. In the beginning planning is time-consuming, even annoying, but eventually your new routine will become a habit. At the end of the month review each goal. Has it been accomplished? Does it need to be restated or is it part of the family routine? Review the goals you listed under each exercise and add them to a new plan of action, replacing any old ones that have been accomplished. Keep the original issues if they are still relevant.

To keep children interested in your plan of action involve them in all areas that pertain to them, such as helping select fruits and favorite vegetables, and refining or revising the snack list. Ask your children to use the Get Fit Log on page 179 whenever you think they, or you, need to review the effectiveness of your plan of action.

I Am a Failure

For most of us a change in diet is an all-or-nothing commitment. We set goals about what we will eat, and how often we will exercise. We practice these goals for a week, maybe more, and then we stop. Our usual response is that we have failed. We feel guilty, and that's the end of our improved health program, that is, until we get worried about our health again. My advice to you is to assume that your goals for improved family health will always be tested and always be in transition. There will be days and weeks you are on target and times when you are not. Just keep going. You are not a failure because you didn't meet a goal. I have never met anyone who is perfect at meeting all their goals. Life gets in the way, and finding time to eat well and get the exercise we need always comes at the expense of something else.

What I love about working with families is that parents are highly motivated to do what is best for their children, and while their own health needs may be put on the back burner the needs of their children are not. Because you are a parent you will probably take this more seriously than if you were doing it just for yourself. You are also setting an example for your child; goals can be hard to meet, but the danger lies not in not living up to the goals but in not setting them at all. Don't get discouraged. Just start over as often as you need.

GET FIT LOG

Use this log to keep track of the foods you eat and the exercise you do over a week. Circle a ▲ each time you eat a serving from one of the food groups. Circle ⑤ each time you do five minutes of physical activity. At the end of the week if you see only a few blanks in the food groups and do at least thirty minutes of physical activity three to five times per week, keep up the good work! If not then try to eat more foods from the missing food groups and make a plan to get the activity you need.

FOOD GROUP	SUNDAY	MONDAY	TUESDAY	WEDNESDAY	THURSDAY	FRIDAY	SATURDAY
Calcium	▲	▲	▲	▲	▲	▲	▲
Protein	▲	▲	▲	▲	▲	▲	▲
Vegetable	▲▲▲	▲▲▲	▲▲▲	▲▲	▲▲▲	▲▲▲	▲▲▲
Fruit	▲	▲	▲	▲	▲	▲	▲
Grain	▲▲▲▲	▲▲▲▲	▲▲▲▲	▲▲▲▲	▲▲▲▲	▲▲▲▲	▲▲▲▲
Minutes of Physical Activity	⑤⑤ ⑤⑤ ⑤⑤	⑤⑤ ⑤⑤ ⑤⑤	⑤⑤ ⑤⑤ ⑤⑤	⑤⑤ ⑤⑤ ⑤⑤	⑤⑤ ⑤⑤ ⑤⑤	⑤⑤ ⑤⑤ ⑤⑤	⑤⑤ ⑤⑤ ⑤⑤

8

≡

Cooking Real Food

As parents we need to find ways to bring some of this (pleasure at the table) back so that our children can have memories of home-cooked food and a family meal.

—LAURIE COLWIN, *JOURNAL OF GASTRONOMY*

People who are really interested in something, who pay attention to the details, who care about food and take the time to make it right, are happier and more satisfied.

—MARY SYLAS WYLIE, *THE FAMILY THERAPY NETWORKER*

When a group of Minneapolis boys and girls were asked what could make eating healthier and easier, they said:

- Make healthful food look and taste better.
- Make healthful food the only available option.
- Make healthful food more convenient.
- Have parents teach what is healthy.
- Make it cool to eat healthfully.

The recipes and shopping advice that follow were designed to make these five points a reality. You'll find recipes for quick delicious snacks that your kids will love and you will feel good about serving. To make serving vegetables easier I've included a simple primer on how to prepare ten of America's favorite veggies and a chart on how to prepare whole grains. To help your family meet its fruit requirement I have included more than ten different ways to serve fruit as a snack or a dessert. All of the recipes that follow are considered Everyday choices unless specified otherwise. Just a few of the desserts are considered a Sometime choice and only two an Occasional choice. In each recipe heading I've included suggestions for what to serve with the recipe to make a meal complete, and after each serving size you'll find a listing of the food groups contained in the recipe.

To make it "cool" to eat healthfully, parents can point out athletes or celebrities who endorse sound health practices, and surround your child with magazines that support good nutrition and provide accurate information about food and fitness.

BE A SMART SHOPPER

To put your child on a proper diet you want to make the usual and customary food she eats naturally low in fat and as dense in nutrients as possible. Such a combination will help her reach and maintain her natural weight, and keep her well nourished. To accomplish this just select food and plan meals based on the Everyday choices described in chapter 6. When you go to the grocery store you may find you need more guidance. Since shopping is where healthy eating starts, you have to have a good knowledge of what to eat every day, occasionally, and sometimes. Here is an aisle-by-aisle guide to help assist you at the grocery store, and a sample grocery list on page 202 to use as a guide.

Aisle by Aisle

Fresh Produce

All fruit and vegetables in this aisle are great sources of fiber and nutrition. Bag salads, cut-up carrot and celery sticks are real convenient time-savers, but they do cost more. If your market has a salad bar, select items that are not marinated, and if you add cheese or egg to the salad remember to count it as a serving of protein—not vegetable.

Deli Counter

There was a time when all deli food was high in fat and sodium but not anymore. In this section look for the items labeled "low-fat." Everyday choices include chicken or turkey breast, rotisserie chicken (try not to eat the skin).

Sometime choices include lean boiled ham, lean beef, turkey ham, turkey pastrami. Occasional choices include regular hot dogs, high-fat luncheon meats, liverwurst, salami, sausages, bacon, refrigerated meals (Lunchables), prepared salads, including potato and macaroni, and dessert puddings.

Dairy/Refrigerator Case

Nestled among the milk, cheese, and yogurt you will find an array of other foods that require refrigeration such as pie crust, biscuits, breakfast pastry, coffee creamer, prepared pudding, nondairy creamer, sour cream substitutes, flavored fruit drinks. Most of these belong in the Sometime and Occasional choices. Only low-fat milk, low-fat cheese, and real fruit juice are on the Everyday choices, as is soft tub margarine, soft butter, and soft tortillas.

Meat/Poultry/Fish

Everyday choices include any plain or unprocessed fish, shellfish, or poultry, including all plain fresh or frozen fish such as shellfish, abalone, clams, crab, imitation crabmeat, mussels, oysters, scallops, lobster, shrimp, and crayfish. Poultry, especially white-meat chicken, cornish hen, wild duck, turkey (preferably not self-basting). Sometime choices include: prebreaded fish, lean cuts of beef (roasts, steak, extra-lean ground beef, stew meat), lean lamb, veal, and pork. Occasional choices: prefried fish, prepared seafood salad, veal breast, bacon, regular ground beef, prime grade and heavily marbled beef, traditional corned beef, salt pork, sausage, short ribs, and spareribs.

Canned/Jarred Foods

Most canned and jarred foods are high in sodium (except for fruit and those that state "no salt"). This is why some of your favorite foods like spaghetti sauce are in the Sometime and not Everyday choices. To keep sodium intake moderate keep snack foods containing more than 500 mg sodium to one per day and prepared entrées or main dishes carrying 800 to 1,000 mg of sodium to one per day. Everyday choices: broth-based soup such as a vegetable or chicken soup, canned chicken, tuna, shrimp, clams, salmon, oysters, and crabmeat packed in water. Fruit canned in its own juice or water. Vegetables canned without salt. Sometime choices: most tomato and spaghetti sauces (particularly meatless tomato sauce), olives, pickles, relishes. Fruit packed in syrup (rinse before serving). Vegetables canned with salt. Occasional choices include: canned stew, canned macaroni, canned hash, cream of cheese soups, creamy chowders, vichysoise.

Oils/Salad Dressings

Everyday choices: canola, corn, olive, safflower, soybean, sunflower, vegetable oil sprays, walnut, any salad dressing made from these oils. Sometime choices: peanut, sesame seed, soybean, cottonseed shortening, partially hydrogenated soybean oil. Any salad dressing made with partially hydrogenated or hydrogenated oil. Occasional choices: coconut, palm, and palm kernel oil.

Cereals

A complete list of Everyday choices is listed in chapter 6 under the grain/starch group. You want to select whole grain cereals as low in added sugar as possible and serve the high-sugar refined cereals as dessert instead of breakfast food.

Snacks/Crackers

Everyday choices are listed in the grain/starch group. Look for items that are naturally low in fat and carry some fiber: flat and crisp breads, plain rice cakes, popcorn cakes, bagel chips are all possible choices. Do buy and keep on hand one or two selections from the Sometime and Occasional choices your child really enjoys. Every child deserves a cookie and a fun food from time to time. Just establish the goal of eating at least five fruits and veg-

etables per day, and serve these higher calorie foods sometimes or occasionally—not every day!

Pastas/Rice

These foods are all naturally low in fat. Try to introduce
your family to more whole grains such as brown rice, bulgur, barley, even whole wheat pasta. Try shopping at your
local health food stores for these items. Whole grains are
sold in bulk and are much, much less expensive than
prepackaged products.

Baked Goods

The bread aisle offers a variety of choices. To reach the
recommendation of three whole grain foods per day for
adults and at least one or more for children try to find a
whole grain bread your family likes. Most bread is naturally low in fat, but heavily refined white breads may be
consumed in excess. A complete list of Everyday choices
is found in the grain/starch group starting on page 117.
Most cakes and breakfast goods such as doughnuts and
commercial muffins are made with partially hydrogenated and hydrogenated oils and carry a lot of sugar,
and are best served as an Occasional choice. Kids tend to
have trouble self-regulating these foods.

Seasonings and Sauces

Most of these foods are used in small amounts and contribute more in the way of flavor than nutrition, and most
of them can be used every day. The only limitation is if
your child is using a high-sodium sauce on every food.

Such a habit provides a lot of sodium and doesn't allow for a varied taste experience.

Frozen Foods

Look for simple unadorned food, including any food listed as an Everyday choice from chapter 6 such as frozen: fruits, vegetables without sauces, stir-fry vegetables with no or low-fat sauces, vegetable-pasta and vegetable-rice combinations without sauces. Look for vegetarian burgers—use these to replace ground beef. Frozen whole grain waffles and bagels are good choices, as are frozen ravioli, pierogi, and tortellini. Some ready-to-heat breakfast and lunch sandwiches can make for a good, quick meal but are too high in calories to be a good snack choice. Frozen juice concentrate such as orange and pineapple are Everyday choices. Fruit blends and fruit drinks are Sometime choices.

DECIDING ON FROZEN OR PREPARED FOODS NOT MENTIONED IN THE FOOD GROUPS

It is impossible to list every frozen and prepared food. They are too numerous, and new products are added constantly. This is where you can use the food label and the nutrition information that preceded each food group in chapter 6 to help you. Ask yourself which food group the item fits into. If it is in the grain/starch group then each serving should contain at least 1 to 2 grams of fiber. If it is a food that fits in the calcium group then each serving should provide 300 mg of calcium, written as 30 percent calcium on the label.

Remember too that frozen main dish meals should be providing the family with about one-third of all their nutrition needs. You can use the same method used to evaluate fast-food meals, on page 145, to assess frozen entrées. Be aware of sodium and the type of fat used in frozen or prepared foods too. Keep saturated fat and partially hydrogenated and hydrogenated fats low, and keep

---

SHOPPING WITH KIDS

Kids will be kids, especially in the grocery store. With a little bit of preplanning and preparation you can take the stress out of shopping with children.

1. If your child is too tired or hungry postpone your trip until after lunch or naptime.

2. Set your own rules. Show your child your list and tell them you plan to buy only what is on the list (unplanned sales and special purchases are an exception). Explain the type of behavior you expect and be specific— sitting in the cart, not wandering or running down the aisles—that sort of thing.

3. Involve your child in the process. Should we buy these bananas or those bananas? Apples or oranges?

4. Explain to your child that you need their cooperation in the store. You may want to offer a reward such as reading a story or playing a game together when you get home.

5. Decide how you will handle free cookies, free food samples, or requests for unplanned purchases—be flexible but don't send confusing messages.

to fewer than 1,000 mg of sodium per main dish, per day. Once you start looking at food labels and become familiar with the food groups and their Everyday choices the job of shopping will become easier.

THE FAMILY MEAL—MAKING IT HEALTHIER

For over twenty years I have been talking to families about what they eat. When young children are in the home many families rely on very familiar and similar meal combinations. Below is a nutrition review of the meal combinations families ask me about most often. With a few alterations any meal can become a healthy meal. In general, you want to emphasize fruit and vegetable servings and keep the protein group and the fat/oil group in its place—not eliminated, but not dominating either.

Pasta and Sauce

To make a spaghetti meal healthier you can experiment with whole wheat pasta, but I will be honest: many young children do not like it, and if it doesn't taste good to your children you shouldn't push it on them (find other ways to offer whole grains). Cook about two ounces of pasta per dinner, toss with olive oil over butter. Serve a meatless sauce on top, or if you include meat, reduce the total amount of meat or sausage you use to 2 to 3 ounces per diner, or try ground turkey instead of ground beef. Serve a salad and a cooked vegetable with the meal. If you serve bread with pasta consider a whole wheat bread. If serving breadsticks try to find one low in fat and made without hydrogenated fat.

Fish

Instead of serving fried fish or fish sticks all the time try the recipe for Oven Fried Fish (page 217) or Poached Fish using the microwave (page 219). Serve 4- to 6-ounce portions to each person. Garnish fish with lemon instead of tartar sauce and serve it with a starch such as rice, noodles, or potato, and two to three vegetables.

Hamburger

Instead of ground beef try ground turkey or even a vegetarian or meatless burger. Use a cooking method such as broiling or a grill that allows the fat to drain away from the meat. Keep to 3 ounces and serve with lettuce and tomato on a soft roll (try to find whole wheat rolls). Use low-fat or soy cheese to make a cheeseburger or skip the cheese altogether and drink a glass of milk for the calcium. Serve Oven Fries, page 234, instead of frozen or deep-fried french fries or potato chips, and serve at least two vegetables with the meal. Pickles, relish, mustard, chopped onion, and ketchup are all acceptable toppings. Skip high-fat toppings such as bacon, sautéed mushrooms, or fried onions.

Hot Dog and Beans

Buy a low-fat hot dog (read labels and find one you like) or try a soy or tofu hot dog. Limit hot dogs to one or two. Buy canned baked beans that contain no saturated fat. If you make your own beans using salt pork, remove it before serving. Serve dark brown bread, corn, peas, or even sauerkraut with the meal. Mustard, ketchup, relish, pickles, and onions can top the hot dog without adding many calories.

Fried Chicken

Count fried chicken as your one serving of fried food for the week. Prepare only one or two pieces of chicken per adult diner. If you can fry the chicken without the skin you will be saving a significant amount of saturated fat. Serve it with a low-fat starch such as baked potato, rice, or noodles, and at least three vegetables. Avoid coleslaw or french fries as side dishes. Or skip deep-fried chicken and try Oven Fried Chicken, on page 212.

Pizza

In my experience kids do not like to modify their pizza. While it would be healthier to add vegetables, don't do it if they will hate it. Instead serve vegetables on the side in the form of a salad or vegetable sticks. Don't buy or cook more pizza than you need. The delicious combination of salt and fat from the melted cheese makes it hard to stop eating when we are no longer truly hungry. Hold off on adding high-fat meat choices too, such as sausage, ground beef, meatballs, pepperoni, or salami. Each small slice of cheese pizza carries at least ten grams of fat per slice, and some commercial pizzas carry much greater amounts. Count pizza as one of your two full-fat cheese selections for the week.

Macaroni and Cheese

Kids love macaroni and cheese, and yes, you can make it healthier by adding slivers of cooked zucchini or peas or bits of carrots. But when I have tried to sneak veggies into the macaroni and cheese my kids hated it. Instead, serve vegetables on the side such as slices of tomato, sliced carrots or cucumber and prepare only as much macaroni and cheese as your family actually needs. If you're making macaroni and cheese for two kids, 8 ounces of cooked noodles should be enough and it will allow room for the important side servings of vegetables.

Tacos

Mexican-flavored foods are a big hit with kids, but ground beef and grated cheese can add lots of fat. Salsa, lettuce, tomato, and soft tortillas are Everyday choices low in fat. When making tacos try using ground turkey instead of ground beef, and try the vegetable burger (in the frozen foods case) at least once to see if you like it. Use only 16 ounces of ground meat to serve four diners and make sure you drain off as much fat as you can before adding seasoning mix or serving. You can even try adding a can of rinsed kidney beans or refried beans into the meat mixture to boost fiber and replace some of the meat. Serve a grain with the meal such as rice or cooked corn, and provide lots of lettuce and chopped tomato. Skip the sour cream but include avocado or homemade guacamole if your kids like it. Soft tortillas are lower in fat than fried tacos, but if your kids like the crisp tacos serve them and count them as your fried food for the week.

Roast Dinner

A roast dinner is a problem on a low-fat diet because the roast, which is the center of the meal, is naturally high in fat. To improve the typical roast menu, whether it be beef, pork, or lamb, allow only 4 ounces of cooked meat for each diner instead of the customary 8 ounces. This may mean you have to freeze half, since most roasts are two to three pounds—enough for eight to ten servings. Make a gravy only after you have removed all the fat on the surface. Serve a starch along with three vegetables such as a salad and two cooked vegetables and a baked fruit dish for dessert.

Steak and Potatoes

Many families love this traditional combination—particularly men. To make it more in line with a low-fat diet examine how much steak you buy for the number of eaters and allow about 4 ounces of cooked meat for each adult. Serve potatoes baked or mashed instead of fries, and in this case count the potato as a starch. Serve a salad and at least two cooked vegetables. Include a loaf of good whole wheat bread to round off the meal.

VEGETABLE PRIMER

I have met mothers who do not know how to bake a potato and fathers who do not know how to make a fruit salad. If children live in a house where the grown-ups don't know how to properly prepare a vegetable or serve fruit the family cannot possibly eat well. Fruit can be served whole, or a fruit salad recipe can be found on page 242.

A basic vegetable guide follows. Steaming is an easy and delicious way to cook vegetables, and next to raw this is the way kids seem to like them

best. To cook, steam in a collapsible steaming bas-
ket if you have one, or use a metal insert with
holes in it set over an inch or two of boiling water.
Or you can place chopped vegetables in an inch of
water, cover, and steam for the recommended
time. The problem with this method is the vegetables on the bottom can be overcooked, but stirring will help. Wash all vegetables and peel any
with tough skins, then cut into even-size pieces.
Cooking times always depend on the size of the
food being cooked, but the suggestions below will
be a good guide. Remove your vegetables immediately when done, toss with a squeeze of fresh
lemon, a little butter, olive oil, or a tablespoon of
grated Parmesan cheese and serve hot.

Asparagus—leave whole, trim tough stems,
steam five minutes.

Beets—cut off stems and leaves, scrub well but
do not peel. Steam whole for forty minutes. (Make
sure you don't steam away all the water.) Run under
cold water and slide skin off with your fingers.

Broccoli—trim stem, cut florets and stem into
quarters. Steam five to seven minutes.

Carrots—trim root, peel skin. Cut into coins,
slices, or steam whole for five to ten minutes,
depending on size of pieces.

Cauliflower—cut into florets, remove hard
core, steam seven to eight minutes.

Corn—husk the corn, place in steamer, and
steam ten minutes.

Green beans—trim off stem end, leave whole
or cut into 2-inch lengths, steam eight to ten minutes.

Potatoes—use small red, new potatoes for steaming. Scrub well, leave whole, steam fifteen to twenty-five minutes. To bake, select an Idaho or russet, scrub, pierce skin with a fork, and bake at 400°F for sixty minutes until done, or microwave on high for three minutes, turn and cook one to two minutes longer until tender when pierced with a fork.

Spinach—trim thick stems, wash very well in several changes of water, use whole leaves, steam five minutes. Spinach will decrease in size by at least half.

Zucchini—thoroughly wash zucchini, trim stem end, cut into even size slices or cubes, steam three to five minutes.

ALTERNATIVES

Just by making simple food substitutions, parents can boost nutrition and save their child from eating thousands of empty calories over the course of a year, and no one in the family will even notice. Here are some suggestions that I use in my house all the time. Give them a try.

Grain Group

Instead of	Substitute with
biscuits	toast or bagel
white rice	brown rice
saltines	Triscuits
french fries	oven-baked fries

frosted cake	angel food cake
chocolate chip cookies	gingersnaps
buttered popcorn	air-popped popcorn

Calcium Group

whole milk	1% milk
regular cheese	low-fat or reduced-fat cheese or "light" mozzarella

Protein Group

ground beef	ground turkey breast or meatless burger meat in frozen food section
regular bologna	low-fat or fat-free bologna
bacon	turkey bacon or Canadian bacon
sausage	low-fat sausage
hot dogs	tofu hot dogs
chicken with skin	skinless chicken
fried chicken	baked or broiled chicken

Fat/Oil/Snack/Sweet/Other Group

stick margarine	low-fat tub margarine
butter	light whipped butter
butter for baking	substitute applesauce for half the amount

oil for frying	broth or nonstick spray
whole milk/cream in soup	evaporated skim milk
sour cream	plain yogurt
mayonnaise in sandwiches	mustard (any type) or salsa
chocolate candy	jelly beans
chocolate chip cookies	gingersnaps
potato chips	carrot sticks
regular soda	plain or flavored seltzer or sparkling water
fruit drinks	fruit juice mixed with sparkling water, half and half

Combination Foods

pepperoni, sausage, or cheese pizza	pizza with vegetables

WHAT AND WHY YOU SHOULD TEACH YOUR KIDS TO COOK

It takes time to teach safe and proper cooking, but if your child is interested and enjoys the process you are spending true "quality time" together and participating in a parent-child tradition that once made children feel "important" in the family. Don't get discouraged if your first efforts take more time than you would like. The more you work with your child the more competent he or she will become.

According to a *Boston Globe* article almost half of children between ages nine and seventeen regularly pre-

pare meals for themselves. That number is up from 15
percent in 1988, and more than a quarter of these children regularly prepare meals for their families, up from 8
percent in 1988. This increase is probably a result of
more dual working families, but I see the change as
potentially positive. Many of today's children do not have
a meaningful way to contribute to the family workload.
Don't blame the kids—we live in one of the wealthiest
countries in the world, and kids don't need to work in the
fields, tend to the animals, or even keep the house clean.
As a result children are missing out on the experience of
having truly meaningful family responsibilities. Such
experience makes children feel competent and good
about themselves. Cooking can be a way for children to
get that experience. Two problems can arise when kids
become family cooks: one is bad nutrition if the cook
does not know how to prepare nutritious food, and the
other is safety. It is a parent's responsibility to teach
kitchen safety and it is their parents who will teach kids
how to cook.

Teach your child how to prepare most of the food
listed below and he will have learned most of the essential
techniques of cooking including: how to read a recipe,
measure ingredients, combine ingredients (mix, stir, beat,
fold), how to sauté, boil, steam, fry, bake, and roast. If you
are not much of a cook yourself the two of you can learn
together. The kitchen is a great place for families to spend
time together, and a delicious hot meal continues to be a
good draw even for a busy teenager. Make sure you
review the safety tips from page 200 with your child
before you start to cook.

Every child by age eighteen should know recipes for
the following: muffins; pasta with a simple homemade

sauce; vegetable or chicken soup; chicken or pot roast, including potatoes and gravy; steamed vegetables; baking powder biscuits; yeast bread; cake from scratch with frosting; white sauce or cheese sauce to top vegetables; fruit salad and vegetable salad; scrambled egg and hard-boiled egg. Last but not least have your child prepare an entire meal, including setting the table and serving it to the family, even invited friends.

COOKING WITH YOUNG CHILDREN

Involve your child in the process and they will be more likely to try new foods.

- A two-year-old can scrub vegetables, tear lettuce, snap green beans, bring ingredients from one place to another.

- A three-year-old can do all that the two-year-old can plus knead and shape dough, pour liquids, mix ingredients, place things in the trash, spread soft spreads.

- A four-year-old can do the above plus peel oranges or hard-cooked eggs. Use a dull, clean scissor to cut parsley, herbs, or chives; mash bananas; set the table.

- A five- and six-year-old can measure ingredients (with supervision), cut with a plastic knife, use an eggbeater.

- A seven- to eight-year-old can do all of the above, plus they can operate a mixer with

Mom close at hand, stir ingredients, pour batter into pans, assemble casseroles.

- A nine- and ten-year-old can cook alongside
  Mom, can learn how to turn the oven on and off,
  and can learn how to use the microwave. They
  should always use safety gloves while carefully
  heating or cooking items in the microwave.

- An eleven- and twelve-year-old can prepare
  foods on the stove top, read recipes, and prepare whole recipes from start to finish.

Teach your children how to clean too; the best
way is to clean as you go.

KITCHEN SAFETY

- Always wash hands using soap and warm
  water before cooking.

- Always wash cutting boards and utensils after
  use.

- Do not cross contaminate food or surfaces
  with dirty hands, or prepare produce and raw
  meat in the same area.

- Always keep food refrigerated until ready to use.

- Use oven mitts instead of pot holders to handle hot pots or pans—including foods that go
  in and out of the microwave. Mitts offer the
  most protection.

- Always turn pot handles into the counter or
  backsplash to prevent spills.

- Always place knives away from the edge or the reach of small children.

- In general, children younger than twelve should not be putting food in and out of a hot oven unsupervised.

- Have a plan for dealing with a kitchen fire or a burn.

- Have a plan for dealing with a cut.

- Wipe spills immediately.

- Do not leave burners unattended.

- Keep hot food hot, cold food cold.

EATING NATURALLY LOW-FAT, NUTRIENT-DENSE FOOD AND MEALS

When planning meals allow for generous servings and portions from the grain/starch, fruit, and vegetable groups. This way family members who need to eat more food can enjoy second servings from the food groups that carry the most nutrition and the lowest amount of fat. Use the sample grocery list on page 202 before shopping. This sample is based on a grocery list that first appeared in the *Nutrition Action Health Letter.* I've used it with individuals to help them organize their shopping. Control the portion sizes from the protein, calcium, fat/oil, and snack/sweet/other groups. In short, what you want to do is eat a bit more "vegetarianlike," making fruits, vegetables, and grains the centerpiece of meals as much as possible. What follows are recipes I've tried and found to be successful with my family. These are kid-friendly foods, not too exotic and definitely not difficult to make.

GROCERY LIST

Vegetables

carrots/celery
spinach/greens/kale
peppers: red/green
broccoli/cauliflower
lettuce/tomatoes
green beans
onions/garlic
potatoes: white and red
winter and summer
squash
other:_____
_____
_____

Fruit

apples/bananas/oranges/
grapefruit/melon/
pineapple/blueberries/
strawberries
other:_____
_____
_____

Deli/Seafood

fish/shellfish
sliced: turkey/chicken/
roast beef
other:_____
_____
_____

Canned Goods

tomatoes/tomato sauce
beans: black beans/
chickpeas/kidney
tuna/salmon/chicken
broth/soup
other:_____
_____
_____

Breakfast Cereal

shredded wheat/
Cheerios/Wheaties
oatmeal/wheat germ
other:_____
_____
_____

Crackers/Snacks

graham crackers/animal
crackers/whole wheat
crackers/flat breads/fig bars
popcorn/peanuts in
shell/raisins
baked tortilla chips
other:_____
_____
_____

Bread

bread: whole wheat,
rye/pita, rolls/English
muffin
other:_____
_____
_____

Dairy

milk: skim/1%
yogurt: low-fat
cheese:Swiss/
cheddar/low-fat cottage
cheese
butter/soft margarine
other:_____
_____
_____

Dry Goods

flour: white/whole wheat
rice: brown/white
beans: lentils/split peas

Oil/Spices/Flavorings

oil: canola/corn/salad
dressing made with liquid
vegetable oil
salsa/low-sodium soy
sauce
peanut butter
honey/syrup/jam
ketchup/mustard
other:_____
_____
_____

Desserts

frozen
yogurt/sorbet/ice milk
other:_____
_____
_____

Drinks

fruit juices: grapefruit
orange/pineapple
club soda: plain/flavored
coffee/tea
other:_____
_____
_____

Frozen

fruit, 100% juice, plain
vegetables, ravioli, pierogi,
burritos
other:_____
_____
_____

GREAT GRAINS

If you can boil water you can cook any grain in the world. Directions for cooking will be included on the package. If you buy in bulk at the health food store use the guidelines below. Serve grains tossed with a little bit of oil, butter, or soft margarine as a side dish or topped with steamed vegetables.

Barley, pearled. Boil in unlimited water or broth for 45 minutes.

Buckwheat (kasha). Cook like white rice.

Bulgur. Cook like brown rice.

Couscous. Boil enough water or broth to cover couscous, pour over couscous, cover and let stand 5 minutes. Fluff before serving.

Rice, white. Combine 1 cup rice, 2 cups water, ½ tsp salt, 1 tsp butter in a 3-quart saucepan. Bring to a boil, stir once, cover, reduce heat to low, and cook 15 to 20 minutes until grain is tender and water is absorbed.

Rice, brown. Follow white rice instructions, cooking for 50 minutes.

Quinoa (pronounced *keenwa*). Cook like white rice.

Wheat berries. Cook like brown rice, test after 45 minutes.

Crispy Stuffed Chicken Thighs with Pasta and Tomatoes

I like to cook with boneless, skinless chicken thighs because they don't dry out as quickly as a chicken breast and they cost less. Serve this with a salad, frozen Italian green beans prepared according to directions, and whole grain bread.

Serves 4; 1 protein, 1 vegetable, 1 grain/starch

8 boneless, skinless chicken thighs, about 1 to 1½ pounds,
    trimmed of all fat
2 tablespoons fresh grated Parmesan cheese
1 teaspoon minced garlic
¾ cup seasoned bread crumbs, divided
2 tablespoons olive oil, divided
1 egg, beaten
14½-ounce can diced, seasoned tomatoes
8 ounces cooked pasta, white or whole wheat

1. Preheat oven to 375°F. Lay the chicken thighs on a cutting board, cover with wax paper, and pound with a heavy spoon or small, heavy pan until flat.

2. Combine the cheese, garlic, ¼ cup of the bread crumbs, and 1 tablespoon oil.

3. Place about 2 tablespoons of the cheese stuffing in the center of each thigh, pull up the sides and secure with a toothpick.

4. Dip each thigh into the egg and roll in the remaining bread crumbs. Place on a baking sheet with the tooth-pick down. Drizzle with oil and bake about 25 minutes. While the chicken bakes heat the tomatoes in a small saucepan until warm.

5. Place the chicken on the pasta, cover with the tomatoes, and serve.

Time-Saving Tip: make double portions of the chicken and freeze before cooking, or if using previously frozen thighs cook completely, cool, and then freeze without the tomatoes or pasta.

French Toast Chicken Pot Pie

I love baked, savory main-dish meat pies, but pie crust—
whether homemade or store bought—carries a lot of fat,
so instead I use slices of firm bread with the crust
trimmed to make it pretty and elegant. I usually leave the
peels on the potato but you can peel them if you like.
Serve with sliced tomatoes or carrot sticks.

Serves 4; 1 protein, 2 vegetables, 1½ grain/starch

3 cups chicken stock
1 pound boneless, skinless chicken breasts or thighs, or 2
    cups cooked diced chicken
2 cups scrubbed white or red potatoes, cut into 1-inch
    cubes
1 cup sliced carrots
salt and pepper
3 teaspoons butter or soft margarine
½ cup all-purpose flour
1 cup frozen peas
½ cup low-fat milk
2 eggs
6 slices white or whole wheat bread, crust trimmed, and
    cut in half (bread that is a bit stale will work
    beautifully)

1. Preheat oven to 375°F. Lightly oil a two-quart baking
    dish and set aside. If using raw chicken, heat the broth
    on medium heat, add the chicken, and cook until
    opaque and firm, about 15 minutes on medium heat.
    Remove from the broth, setting broth aside. Cool the
    chicken and cut into 1-inch cubes.

2. While the chicken cools, melt the butter in a large

pot, add the flour, stir, and cook for 3 minutes. Pour in the reserved stock and continue to cook until the sauce thickens, about 3 minutes.

3. Add the potatoes and carrots to the thickened stock and cook for 3 to 6 minutes or longer until tender. Remove from the heat, add the cooked chicken, and peas. Taste and season with salt and pepper.

4. Pour into prepared pan.

5. In a shallow bowl, whisk together the milk and eggs. Dip each slice of bread in the mixture until soaked, about 20 seconds. Arrange the slices on the casserole. Overlap if needed, but try to cover as much of the surface as you can. Bake for 20 minutes until top is golden and gravy bubbles. Serve hot.

Chicken and Barley

You might think the seasonings called for here would be too much for children. I have served this dish many times and to different children, and it has always been a hit. Serve with a salad or cut-up vegetables and cooked peas or green beans and fruit for dessert.

Serves 4; 1 protein, 1 vegetable, 2 grain/starch

vegetable oil spray
1½ pounds chicken parts (thigh, leg, or breast, skin removed), patted dry and seasoned with salt and pepper
¼ pound sweet Italian sausage, casing removed and crumbled or chopped
1 small onion, chopped
1 red pepper, seeded and diced
3 cloves garlic, finely chopped
2 cups pearl barley
1 teaspoon ground cumin
½ teaspoon chili powder
½ teaspoon turmeric (optional)
1 bay leaf
14½-oz can peeled, crushed tomatoes
2½ cups water

1. Spray a heavy soup pot or Dutch oven lightly with the vegetable oil spray and sauté the sausage until brown, about 3 minutes. Remove the sausage to a platter. Add the chicken and cook the chicken pieces for about 10 minutes, turning often, or until golden on all sides. Remove the chicken, set aside, and drain the oil from the pan.

2. Lightly spray the pan again with vegetable oil and sauté the onion, pepper, and garlic for about 2 minutes. Stir in the barley, add seasonings, the tomatoes, and water. Bring to a boil, cover, and reduce the heat to a simmer. Cook for 20 minutes. Add more water if it looks dry.

3. Add the chicken and sausage and cook an additional 25 minutes until chicken is completely cooked and barley is tender. If the barley looks dry add ½ cup more water. Serve hot in warm bowls.

Turkey Vegetable Soup

Years ago I use to make this soup only with ground beef. When I refrigerated the leftovers there was always a thick skim of solid fat on the surface, easy to remove when cold but easy to eat when hot. We switched to ground turkey with delicious, lower-fat results. Serve with whole grain bread or rolls and fruit for dessert.

Serves 4; 1 protein, 2 vegetables

vegetable oil spray
1 pound ground turkey
1 small onion, chopped
2 cans beef broth
1 32-ounce can chopped tomatoes
2 cups cubed potatoes, about 1 pound
1 cup chopped carrots
½ cup diced celery
1 bay leaf
6 whole peppercorns

1. Lightly coat a large heavy soup pot or Dutch oven with vegetable oil. Sauté the turkey along with the onion and 1 tablespoon of the beef broth for 2 to 3 minutes or until onion is translucent and soft.

2. Stir in remaining ingredients. Cook on medium high heat until it almost comes to a boil. Reduce heat to low, cover, and simmer at least 20 minutes. Serve hot.

Turkey Chili

Many kids like traditional chili, but as a nutritionist I like this version better because it combines beans and grains and calls for lower-fat meat. Serve with cooked corn and a lettuce-tomato salad.

Serves 4; 1 protein, 1 vegetable, 2 grain/starch

2 tablespoons canola oil
1 small onion, chopped
½ pound ground turkey
14-ounce can chicken broth
1½ cup water
1 tablespoon chili powder
2 cloves garlic, minced
1 teaspoon cumin (optional)
1 15½-ounce can red kidney beans, drained and rinsed
1 6-ounce can tomato paste
½ cup pearl barley or bulgur
3 cups cooked rice or macaroni

1. In a large, heavy soup pot sauté the onions in the oil until tender, about three minutes. Add the ground turkey and sauté until no longer pink, about 7 to 8 minutes. Drain fat.

2. Add all remaining ingredients. Bring to a boil, stir, and reduce heat immediately. Cover and cook 30 minutes, stirring occasionally. Remove cover and cook an additional 15 minutes until grains are tender. Serve hot over rice or macaroni.

Oven-Fried Chicken

Fried chicken is delicious but too high in fat to be served frequently. This is a yummy alternative to fried chicken, but don't bother to tell anyone you use yogurt to make it crisp and tender. Serve this with at least two of your family's favorite vegetables, or roast carrots and onions right alongside the potatoes while the chicken cooks.

Serves 4; 1 protein, ¼ calcium, 1 grain/starch

6 to 8 chicken thighs, skinned
2 cups plain yogurt
1 cup seasoned bread crumbs or crushed cornflakes
2 teaspoons olive oil
4 baking potatoes, scrubbed and cut in half

1. Preheat oven to 350°F. Rinse and pat dry the chicken. Roll in the yogurt, coating the chicken generously. Dip in the bread crumbs or cornflakes. Place on lightly oiled baking dish. Add potatoes. Drizzle the chicken and potatoes with the oil.

2. Bake 45 minutes. Chicken should be crispy and potatoes tender when pierced with a fork.

Pork, Beef, or Chicken Oriental Stir-Fry with Vegetables over Rice

Children either like the taste of soy sauce and Asian food or they don't. My children did not acquire a taste for it until age ten. It is worth a try because stir-fry is a low-fat, simple way to serve vegetables.

Serves 4; 1 protein, 1½ vegetables, 2 to 3 grain/starch

12 ounces lean pork, beef, or chicken
1 thick slice peeled ginger root (available in most
    produce sections)
2 tablespoons canola vegetable oil
8 ounces Chinese pea pods
1 cup thinly sliced carrots
1 8-ounce can sliced water chestnuts, rinsed (available in
    most supermarkets)
4 to 6 cups cooked white rice
Marinade
1 tablespoon cornstarch
1½ tablespoons soy sauce
Sauce
1 cup chicken broth
2 tablespoons soy sauce
1 tablespoon rice wine (available in most supermarkets)
1 teaspoon sugar
2 tablespoons cornstarch

1. Combine cornstarch and soy sauce. Slice beef, pork, or chicken into ¼-inch-thick slices and add to marinade—set aside.

2. In a medium-size glass bowl combine all the sauce ingredients and set aside.

3. In a large saucepan or wok heat 1 tablespoon of the oil, add the ginger and the prepared meat. Cook until done, about 4 minutes. Remove and set aside. Discard the ginger.

4. Add remaining oil, pea pods, carrots, and water chestnuts. Cook until tender, about 3 to 5 minutes. Add the sauce and cook for 3 minutes, stirring often until it starts to thicken. Add the meat and cook until hot and well blended, and vegetables are tender but not overdone. Serve over the cooked rice.

Vegetable Beef Stew

Stew can be made in advance and reheated when you need it. Cut the beef into small pieces so the meat is well distributed throughout the stew. Serve this with sliced tomatoes and whole wheat rolls or bread.

Serves 4; 1 protein, 2 vegetables

16 ounces beef stew trimmed of fat, cut into 16 to 20 small cubes
¼ cup flour
salt and pepper
1 tablespoon canola oil
1 small onion, chopped
1 bay leaf
2 carrots, peeled and cut into coins, about 1 cup
2 small all-purpose potatoes, (about 1½ cups when peeled and chopped)
1 cup frozen green peas, thawed, or 1 cup chopped green beans, fresh or frozen

1. Preheat oven to 350°F. Place the meat and flour in a plastic bag, season with salt and pepper, and shake until the meat is coated. Heat the oil in a large stew pot or Dutch oven. Shake excess flour off the beef and add to the hot oil and brown on all sides for about 3 minutes.

2. Pour enough water into the pot (about 2 cups) to cover the beef by at least 1 inch. Add the onion and bay leaf. Bring to a boil, then remove from heat and cover. Transfer to the hot oven and bake for at least two hours. Check every half hour, add more water, about ½ cup at a time if the liquid cooks away.

3. Fifteen minutes before you are ready to serve, peel
   and chop the potatoes into ½-inch cubes. Add to the
   pot along with the carrots. Cook for 15 minutes or
   until potatoes and carrots are tender but not mushy.
   Add peas or green beans 5 minutes before you serve,
   and continue to cook until they are hot and tender.
   Remove from the oven and serve hot.

Oven Fried Fish

Many people tell me they have been served fish that is dry, overcooked, and smelly so often that they have learned to hate it. This recipe is delicious, easy, and almost foolproof. Use fresh fish if you can get it or frozen, defrosted fillets. Serve it with rice, a tossed salad, cooked peas, and steamed carrots.

Serves 4; 1 protein

1 pound haddock fillets
½ cup milk
¼ teaspoon paprika
salt
pepper
1 cup seasoned bread crumbs in a shallow bowl or plastic
   bag
1 tablespoon olive oil

1. Set oven rack in the top third of oven, but not at the broil level. Preheat oven to 550°F. Pour the milk into a bowl and add the seasonings to the milk.

2. Cut the fish fillets into serving-size pieces. Dip fish into the milk, then into the crumbs. Evenly coat each piece of fish with the crumbs.

3. Arrange the fish on a lightly oiled baking pan. Drizzle with the oil. Bake in the hot oven for 8 to 12 minutes. The crumbs should be golden brown and the fish should flake easily when tested with a fork.

Tuna Rice Casserole

I always have the ingredients for this simple but kid-pleasing dinner on hand. My kids prefer it with white rice, but you can try it with brown rice too—your family might just enjoy it. Serve with sliced tomatoes and raw carrot sticks. Try serving Fruit Clafouti, page 244, for dessert.

Serves 4; 1 protein, 1 vegetable, 1½ grain/starch

1½ cups cooked brown or white rice
1 6-ounce can tuna in water
2 cups frozen peas
4 ounces grated low-fat cheddar cheese

1. Preheat oven to 350°F. Lightly oil a 2-quart casserole dish. Prepare rice according to directions. Once cooked, spread rice evenly in prepared pan. Sprinkle tuna and canned liquid over rice.

2. Distribute peas along the outside edge of dish and sprinkle cheese over entire dish.

3. Bake in preheated oven 10 to 15 minutes until cheese is melted and peas are cooked.

Poached Fish

The microwave oven makes the ideal cooking vehicle for tender, moist fish. It is just like poaching, only easier. I particularly like tuna, salmon, and swordfish prepared this way. Serve fish with a baked potato, whole wheat bread, steamed green beans, and fresh sliced tomatoes.

Serves 4; 1 protein

16 to 20 ounces fish steaks, cut into serving pieces
    (shark, tuna, salmon, swordfish, or a combination of
    fish steaks)
salt and pepper
lemon slices

1. Arrange the fish on a microwave-safe dish so the fish is distributed evenly. Season with salt and pepper. Cover with microwave-safe plastic wrap. Cook on high for 4 minutes. Rotate and cook 2 minutes more. Rest for 1 minute. Check the fish. It should feel firm and flake when pulled with a fork. Serve hot with fresh lemon.

Mexican Lasagna

In our house we love the taste of Mexican food, and while tacos are fun I like this alternative especially because I can make it in advance. Serve it with rice, a lettuce and tomato salad, and fruit for dessert.

Serves 4; 1 protein, 1 grain/starch, 1 vegetable, ½ calcium

1 16-ounce can vegetarian refried beans
1 16-ounce jar prepared salsa
3 10-inch or 6 5-inch soft flour tortillas, whole wheat or
   white or a combination
1 cup frozen whole-kernel corn
1 cup (about 4 ounces) grated cheese such as Mexican
   blend or Monterey Jack

1. Preheat the oven to 350°F. Lightly oil a two-quart casserole dish. Mix the refried beans with ⅔ of the prepared salsa. Line the dish with one or two tortillas. Spread ½ the refried bean mixture evenly over the tortilla(s) in the prepared pan. Top with ½ the corn and ⅓ of the cheese. Repeat another layer, beginning with the tortilla(s), then the bean mixture, corn, and cheese. Top with the remaining tortilla(s), the remaining plain salsa, and the remaining grated cheese.

2. Cover with foil and cook in preheated oven. Bake 25 minutes or until cheese melts and is bubbly. Serve hot.

Pasta, Cheese, and Vegetable Casserole

Most kids are purists about their macaroni and cheese, but you might find your kids will try and actually like this combination if you call it by a different name—mine did. Serve it with vegetable sticks and whole wheat bread, fruit for dessert.

Serves 2; 2 grain/starch, ½ protein, 1 calcium, 1 vegetable

8 ounces cooked elbow macaroni
2 tablespoons cornstarch
2 cups low-fat milk
1 cup grated reduced-fat cheese, divided
1 10-ounce package frozen green vegetable (chopped
   spinach, peas, chopped broccoli, french-style green
   beans, thawed and drained if necessary)

1. Cook the pasta according to directions. Lightly oil a two-quart casserole dish and set aside.

2. Combine the cornstarch and milk in a heavy saucepan. Bring to a boil, reduce heat, and cook 1 to 2 minutes until it starts to thicken. Stir in the cheese and keep stirring until melted.

3. Combine the cheese and the macaroni. Pour one-third of the macaroni in the prepared dish. Top with one-half of the vegetables and repeat, finishing with a layer of macaroni. Bake for 15 minutes and serve while hot.

IT'S A WRAP

Pita bread, soft tortillas, and flat bread make wonderful alternatives to sliced bread. Place any of your favorite low-fat sliced meats along with thinly sliced vegetables such as peppers, carrots, even cucumber, crisp lettuce, and tomato, a smidge of mayonnaise or a hearty dose of mustard in the middle of a pita pocket, soft tortilla, or rectangle of "wrap" bread (try whole wheat if you can find it). Roll the whole thing up, wrap it in foil or wax paper, and you have a great lunch. Hold off on tomatoes or other wet ingredients if you are not eating it right away.

To make a hot wrap put any meat and veggie combination in the middle of the flat bread, roll, and wrap in foil. Heat for 10 minutes at 350°F and eat warm. To microwave: place on a microwave-safe plate with plastic wrap and heat on high for 20 to 30 seconds and eat warm.

Simple Calzone

Make these ahead of time and keep refrigerated up to 12 hours before cooking, or wrap in plastic wrap and freeze for up to 3 months, thaw before cooking. Serve as you would a sandwich, with soup, vegetable sticks, and a glass of milk or juice.

Makes 1 calzone that serves 4; 2 grain/starch, 1 protein

1 pound frozen bread dough, thawed (try whole wheat if you can find it)
1 teaspoon mayonnaise
1 tablespoon mustard
2 ounces grated cheese
2 ounces lean sliced chicken, turkey, or ham
½ green pepper, sliced very thin (optional)
1 small onion, sliced very thin (optional)

1. Preheat oven to 350°F. Roll the defrosted dough out to an 8-by-10-inch rectangle. Spread the dough with the mayonnaise and mustard. Arrange the cheese and meat evenly over the dough. Keep one edge (about 1 inch) clear of ingredients.

2. Roll the dough, starting at the opposite side of the clean edge, until it is rolled tight into a long tubelike shape. Place on a lightly oiled baking sheet. Let rise in a draft-free spot for 20 minutes. (Or wrap in plastic and freeze or loosely wrap in plastic, refrigerate, and let rise on baking sheet for up to 12 hours while refrigerated.)

3. Bake in preheated oven for 20 minutes, until golden brown and the roll sounds hollow when tapped. Allow to cool for 5 to 10 minutes and serve warm.

Mexican Pizza

Most kids love the flavor of Mexican food. Salsa is a nutritious, naturally low-fat food, and when you use it as a topping on whole grain crackers you are providing your child with important and good-tasting nutrition.

Serves 2; 1 grain/starch, 1 vegetable, ¼ calcium

12 whole wheat snack crackers (Triscuits are best)
½ cup prepared salsa
¼ cup grated low-fat cheese

1. Arrange the crackers on a microwave-safe plate. Place a small spoonful of salsa on each cracker and sprinkle the cheese on top.

2. Microwave on high for 10 to 15 seconds (time will vary, depending on oven and number of crackers cooked). The cheese should melt. Serve warm.

Pizza Tortilla

You can serve this open like a pizza or fold it in half and eat it on the run. Either way it is delicious.

Serves two; 1 grain/starch, 1 vegetable, ¼ calcium

2 soft flour tortillas, white or whole wheat
¼ cup prepared pizza sauce or canned tomato sauce
½ cup grated vegetables (carrots, onion, zucchini, mushrooms) (optional)
¼ cup (about 1 ounce) grated mozzarella cheese
pinch of dried oregano (optional)

1. Arrange the tortillas on a microwave-safe plate. Divide and spread the sauce evenly over each tortilla. Top with equal amounts of grated vegetables (if using them), followed by the cheese and oregano (if using it).
2. Cook in the microwave oven on high for 30 seconds until cheese is melted. Serve warm.

226FiT KiDS

English Muffin Mock Pizza

When I was a kid I loved this recipe for "mock pizza." It can be a good snack, but most of the time we ate it as a sandwich. Follow the same directions for Pizza Tortilla only substitute two halves of a toasted English muffin, preferably whole wheat, for the tortilla. Cook in the microwave as described above, or under the broiler for two minutes until the cheese melts.

AFTERSCHOOL OR MIDDAY SNACKS

- Half a bagel topped with 1 ounce melted low-fat cheese.
- Tortilla folded over low-fat cheese and salsa, heated 30 seconds in the microwave.
- Whole grain crackers and a cup of fruit yogurt.
- Toasted bread, spread with peanut butter and thin slices of banana.
- Toasted English muffin topped with ½ ounce sliced turkey, sliced tomato, and good mustard.
- Cucumber slices topped with a thin spread of peanut butter.
- Whole grain muffin and a glass of milk.
- Carrot sticks and favorite salad dressing for dip.
- Fruit salad or cubes of fresh fruit.

Popovers

Surprise your family with a batch of these delightful, puffy treats. Despite what you might think, they are neither hard to make nor high in calories or fat. The trick to a puffy popover is preheating the oven and baking pan. Serve with soup instead of bread or at breakfast along with sliced fruit and a glass of milk.

Makes 12 small popovers; 1 grain/starch per popover

1¼ cup milk
1 teaspoon vegetable oil
2 eggs
1 cup whole wheat pastry flour (or a combination of
    whole wheat and all-purpose flour)
¼ teaspoon salt

1. Preheat the oven to 450°F. Grease a twelve-cup muffin tin with vegetable oil spray and preheat in the oven while you prepare the batter.

2. Whisk together the milk, oil, and eggs. Combine the flour and salt and sprinkle over the egg mixture and fold until just blended.

3. Fill the warm muffin tin ¾ full and bake at 450°F for 10 minutes. Reduce the heat to 350°F and cook 25 minutes more. Do not open the oven until they have cooked for at least 30 minutes or the change in temperature will cause them to deflate. Serve immediately with good jam or honey.

Cinnamon Honey Bran Bread

This is delicious hot out of the oven, but it actually tastes better the next morning toasted for breakfast.

Makes one loaf, 12 slices; 1 grain/starch per slice

1½ cup low-fat milk
⅓ cup honey
1 cup unprocessed bran
½ cup brown sugar
1 teaspoon cinnamon
¼ teaspoon ground nutmeg
⅔ cup whole wheat pastry flour
1 cup all-purpose flour
⅓ cup toasted wheat germ
2 teaspoons baking soda
¼ teaspoon salt
1 egg, beaten
3 teaspoons canola oil
½ cup raspberries or blueberries, fresh or frozen, or
    seedless raisins (optional)

1. Preheat oven to 350°F. Lightly oil a 9-by-5-inch loaf pan. Mix together the milk, honey, and bran. Set aside.

2. In a large bowl combine the brown sugar, cinnamon, nutmeg, whole wheat and white flour, wheat germ, baking soda, and salt. Blend with a fork to combine all of the ingredients.

3. Pour the milk mixture over the dry ingredients. Add the egg and oil and stir with a spoon until well blended. Fold in the fruit (if using it) after the batter is blended.

4. Pour into the prepared pan and bake for 50 minutes or until a knife comes out clean when inserted into the center. Remove from pan and allow to cool for 10 minutes before slicing.

Bran Muffins

Bran muffins are very good for the whole family, but the truth is kids don't usually like them as much as blueberry or cinnamon muffins—unless they are hot out of the oven. This recipe is based on Fabulous Five-Week Fiber Muffins in Susan Purdy's *Have Your Cake and Eat It Too*. The beauty of these muffins is that you prepare the batter ahead and bake only what you need, keeping the remaining batter refrigerated for up to five weeks. This way you can serve your kids a warm bran muffin whenever you want.

Makes 18 muffins; 1 grain/starch per muffin

1 cup boiling water
2 cups All-Bran cereal or unprocessed bran
¾ cup granulated sugar
¼ cup vegetable oil
2 eggs
¾ cup old-fashioned rolled oats
¼ cup toasted wheat germ
1½ cups all-purpose flour
1 cup King Arthur White Whole Wheat Flour
2½ teaspoons baking soda
½ teaspoon salt
¾ teaspoon cinnamon
2 cups buttermilk*
½ cup seedless raisins (optional)
paper muffin-cup liners with aluminum covers
granulated sugar

---

*Instant buttermilk powder can be found next to dry milk in the store. It's ideal to keep on hand for this recipe and to use in any pancake or biscuit recipe for a change of pace.

1. Preheat the oven to 350°F. Pour the boiling water over the bran, stir, and set aside to cool about 10 minutes.

2. In a large bowl combine the sugar, oil, and eggs and mix until well blended. Add all of the remaining ingredients, including the soaked bran, and raisins if using them.

3. Cover and refrigerate up to five weeks or scoop out ⅓ cup batter without stirring and pour into muffin cup liner set in aluminum cover. Set on a baking sheet. Sprinkle with some of the sugar and bake for 20 minutes.

Variations

Right before baking stir in 1 tablespoon fresh blueberries, dried cranberries, or chopped, peeled apple. Bake as directed.

Basic Muffins

I almost never make the same muffins twice. I like the variety and taste of combining different grains and flour. You can do the same, just substitute wheat germ, whole wheat flour, bran flakes, or even oatmeal flakes for some of the all-purpose flour. But to keep your muffins light and airy use all-purpose white flour for half the amount of flour called for. If you want a fruit muffin try any of the optional fruit additions I suggest below.

Makes 12 muffins; 1 grain/starch per muffin

2 cups flour (1 cup white plus any combination
      suggested above)
½ cup granulated sugar
4 teaspoons baking powder
¼ teaspoon salt
1 egg
3 tablespoons vegetable oil
1 teaspoon vanilla
1 cup plain yogurt, milk, or buttermilk
1 very ripe banana, mashed, or ½ cup fresh or frozen
      blueberries or raspberries (optional)
granulated sugar (optional) for sprinkling

1. Preheat the oven to 375°F and line twelve muffin cups with paper liners. Combine the flour, sugar, baking powder, and salt and blend well.

2. In a separate bowl mix until well blended the egg, vegetable oil, vanilla, and yogurt or milk, and banana if using it. (Don't add the berries yet or they will turn the whole batter purple.) Pour the wet ingredients over the dry and blend gently until all the ingredients

are moistened. It's okay if there are a few lumps in the batter. If adding berries fold them in now.

3. Pour batter into muffin cups. Sprinkle with sugar if you are using it. Bake 12 to 15 minutes until golden and cake tester comes out clean when inserted. Remove from the muffin tin and serve warm.

Carrot Muffins

Most children enjoy the taste of carrots. When cooked in a muffin they make a soft, tender, and of course nutritious snack and breakfast treat.

Makes 12 muffins; 1 grain/starch per muffin

1½ cups flour
1 teaspoon baking powder
1 teaspoon baking soda
1 teaspoon cinnamon
¼ teaspoon nutmeg
2 eggs
¾ cup granulated sugar
5 tablespoons vegetable oil
¼ cup milk
1½ cups grated carrot
¼ cup chopped walnuts, ¼ cup raisins (optional)
confectioners' sugar (optional)

1. Preheat oven to 375°F. Combine the flour, baking powder, baking soda, cinnamon, and nutmeg. Blend well and set aside.

2. Mix together the eggs and the sugar. Add the oil and milk and the grated carrots. Blend well. Pour wet ingredients over the dry ingredients and blend until ingredients are moistened. Fold in the nuts and raisins if using them.

3. Bake 18 to 20 minutes until golden or test with a cake tester. Dust with the confectioners' sugar if desired and serve warm.

Oven Fries

Almost everybody likes a hot snack better than a cold one. There is no reason you have to serve these fries just at meals. They make a good afternoon snack as well as a nice accompaniment to sandwiches and soup or stew.

Serves 4; 1 grain/starch or 1 vegetable per serving

4 Idaho or russet potatoes, peeled or unpeeled, and cut
   into ¼-inch-thick french fries
1 tablespoon canola oil
salt to taste

1. Preheat oven to 400°F. Place the prepared potatoes in a plastic bag, add the oil, and toss the potatoes in the oil so all sides are coated.
2. Bake in the preheated oven for 10 minutes. Turn and continue cooking until crisp. Sprinkle with salt and serve with ketchup or salsa.

Variation: Sweet Potato Fries

Wash and peel two large sweet potatoes and proceed exactly as above.

EATING ON THE RUN

If your family is constantly on the go and it leads more than once per week to eating high-fat, and not-so-nutritious food, then you need to make changes. When eating at a fast-food restaurant choose the plain hamburger or small cheeseburger and small fries. Drink milk or juice and bring along a bag of carrot sticks and fruit for dessert. If you need to rely on frozen dinners choose one that meets the suggestion from page 141 in chapter 6. Otherwise rely on homemade sandwiches made from low-fat deli meats and snacks that are from the Everyday choices. Just because you are busy does not mean you can forget about healthy eating. Instead you must think ahead and have food on hand that will fit your lifestyle.

NO-TIME-TO-COOK BREAKFASTS

Whole grain cereal with low-fat milk, fresh fruit, and a drizzle of honey remains our family's favorite no-cook breakfast, but in case cereal becomes boring consider these alternatives:

- Combine equal amounts of any combination of yogurt, juice, and whole fruit in a blender. Blend 10 to 20 seconds and drink immediately.
- Melt cheese over an English muffin or bagel half.
- Spread peanut butter on bread (or a hot dog roll), wrap around a banana, and eat like a hot dog.
- Frozen whole grain waffle toasted and topped with yogurt and fruit.
- Cottage cheese on fresh fruit.
- Stuff a whole wheat pita bread with cheese and thin slices of apple. Heat in the microwave 30 to 40 seconds.
- Mix cereal with yogurt and fruit.

- Tortilla wrapped around scrambled eggs.
- Bagel topped with cottage cheese, a sprinkle of cinnamon, and thin apple slices.

Oatmeal Pancakes

These are a delicious alternative to plain pancakes based on Marion Cunningham's recipe in the *Breakfast Book*. For best results you need to soak the oatmeal the night before but if you forget they can be made without soaking; the batter will be thinner and runny but still delicious.

Makes 16 4-inch pancakes; 1 grain/starch per pancake

⅔ cup oatmeal
2 cups sour milk*
½ cup all-purpose flour
½ cup whole wheat pastry flour
¼ teaspoon salt
1 teaspoon baking soda
1 tablespoon granulated sugar
1 egg
2 tablespoons canola oil

1. The night before sour the milk and add the oatmeal. Cover and keep refrigerated. The next morning combine all the dry ingredients and set aside. In a medium-size bowl beat the egg and add the flour mixture along with the milk/oatmeal mixture. Stir until well blended.

2. Pour ⅓ cup batter on a hot griddle, flip when bubbles form. Serve hot with good syrup.

---

*To sour milk add 1 tablespoon white vinegar to each cup of milk called for. Let sit for 10 minutes before using.

Best Breakfast Puff

Years ago my sister taught me this recipe, and I have used it hundreds of times in my own kitchen. Serve it with a cup of orange juice or milk.

Serves 4; ¼ protein, ¼ calcium, 1 grain/starch

2 tablespoons butter
1 cup milk
4 eggs
1 cup all-purpose flour

1. Preheat oven to 400°F. Place 1 tablespoon butter each in two 1-quart ovenproof casseroles and place in warm oven to melt. While butter melts beat together the eggs and milk until well blended. Pour over the flour and blend with a fork, breaking up any lumps.
2. Remove warm dishes from oven. Swirl butter to coat the edges. Divide the batter equally between each dish. Bake in hot oven 20 minutes. Serve with syrup.

Variation: Blueberry or Apple Puff

Before baking, pour ¼ cup frozen or fresh blueberries or peeled chopped apples on top of the batter in each dish and bake as directed.

Overnight French Toast

If you have two working parents or children who catch an early school bus, breakfast must be well organized or the morning can turn into chaos. I love this recipe because it makes a great warm breakfast and best of all you assemble it the night before and it cooks while the family gets ready for the day. Serve with juice in the morning or a grapefruit half.

Serves 4; 1 protein, 2 grain/starch, ¼ calcium

1 cup milk
6 eggs
8 slices bread, white, whole wheat, or a combination
syrup

Beat together the eggs and milk. Arrange the bread in a lasagna-type pan. Pour the milk mixture over the bread and let sit covered in the refrigerator overnight. In the morning set the oven to 350°F and place the dish in the cold oven. Bake 25 to 30 minutes until fluffy and lightly browned. Serve with syrup.

Raspberry Crumble Bars

These really are crumbly, but they taste so good they are worth messy fingers. They are best when prepared ahead and allowed to cool before serving. Serve as you would any cookie, with a glass of cold milk.

Makes 9 bars; 1 bar equals 1 grain/starch; a Sometime choice

1 cup whole wheat pastry flour
1 cup rolled oats or crushed Wheatabix cereal (found in most cereal aisles)
¼ cup softened butter or tub margarine
¼ cup orange juice
⅓ cup brown sugar
¼ teaspoon baking powder
½ cup raspberry jam
8-inch-square baking pan

1. Preheat the oven to 350°F. Use a spoon to combine all ingredients, except the jam, in a medium-size bowl until the mixture starts to hold together like a crumbly cookie dough.

2. Press about ⅔ of the mixture into a lightly oiled 8-by-8-inch pan, covering the entire bottom of the pan.

3. Mix the jam with a spoon to make it easier to spread and drop by spoonfuls onto the batter, distributing it as evenly as possible over the mixture. Take the remaining flour mixture and spread it over the jam. It will not cover it completely but try to cover it evenly.

4. Bake for 20 minutes until golden and the jam bubbles. Allow to cool for 10 minutes before cutting. The bars will fall apart easily until they cool completely. Enjoy!

Blackened Banana

This has been a favorite in our house since my children were born.

Serves 1; 1 fruit (½ calcium if served with ½ cup yogurt)

1 banana, peel on
plain yogurt, frozen yogurt, or ice milk

1. Prick the skin of the banana with a fork. Cook on a microwave-safe plate for 2 minutes or until the banana is soft, hot, and the skin starts to darken.

2. Scrape the soft, hot banana from the skin with a spoon into a bowl. Serve right away like pudding with yogurt or ice milk if desired.

Pumpkin Pudding

If your family enjoys pumpkin pie at Thanksgiving they will love this all year long. It is packed with fiber, calcium, and vitamin A.

Serves 6; ½ calcium, 1 vegetable; a Sometime choice

15-ounce can pumpkin
2 eggs
12-ounce can evaporated skim milk
1 cup sugar
¾ cup flour
¾ teaspoon baking powder
½ teaspoon baking soda
½ teaspoon cinnamon
½ teaspoon ginger
½ teaspoon nutmeg

1. Preheat the oven to 350°F. Lightly oil a 3-quart casserole or soufflé dish. In a large bowl mix together the pumpkin and the eggs until smooth and well blended. Whisk in the milk.

2. Measure all the dry ingredients and add to pumpkin mixture. Blend thoroughly. Pour into prepared pan and bake for 40 to 50 minutes until set. Serve warm with vanilla frozen yogurt.

Fruit Salad

If your children are not apt to eat a piece of whole fruit on their own, try serving a fruit salad. The convenience and attractiveness of a fruit salad will make it disappear. Use any three of the following fruits to make a salad for two.

Serves 2; 2 fruit per serving

1 navel orange, peeled and cut into wedges
1 ripe papaya, peeled, seeded, and cut into cubes
1 apple, seeds and core removed. If peeled, dip in lemon
   to prevent browning.
1 banana, peeled, cut into slices, dipped in lemon to
   prevent browning
1 kiwi fruit, peeled and cut into cubes
1 cup red or green grapes, washed and sliced in half
1 cup fresh blueberries
1 cup fresh strawberries, hulled and sliced in half
1 teaspoon lemon juice or orange juice

Choose any combination of fruits. Combine the fruit with the lemon or orange juice, cover, and refrigerate until ready to use. Use within 12 hours.

Fruit Crumble

This is a delicious dessert that can be made with any fruit in season or a canned fruit or a combination of fruits.

Serves 4; 1 fruit and 1 grain/starch per serving; a Sometime choice

1 cup whole wheat pastry flour
2 tablespoons toasted wheat germ
⅔ cup granulated sugar
1 tablespoon melted butter
2 tablespoons milk
1 tablespoon vegetable oil
2 cups chopped seeded fruit such as apples, berries, peaches, pears, or 1 15.25-ounce can sliced, unsweetened fruit

1. Preheat oven 350°F. Combine dry ingredients with a fork. Mix together wet ingredients (but not fruit) and pour over flour mixture. Blend until it resembles a crumbly cookie dough.

2. Pour fruit into a lightly oiled 1-quart ovenproof dish. Sprinkle the topping over the fruit. Bake 15 minutes until topping is lightly browned. Serve warm with plain or vanilla yogurt or low-fat frozen yogurt.

Fruit Clafouti

Traditionally, clafouti was made with cherries, but it is delicious prepared with any fruit or fruit combination. Canned fruit packed in juice can be used instead of fresh fruit.

Serves 4; 1½ fruit, ¼ calcium, ½ grain/starch

3 cups prepared fruit such as fresh or frozen berries of
    any type, peeled sliced peaches, peeled sliced apples,
    peeled sliced pears
3 tablespoons granulated sugar
1 cup milk
2 eggs
1 teaspoon vanilla
½ cup all-purpose flour
¼ cup whole wheat pastry flour
¼ teaspoon salt
¼ teaspoon nutmeg

1. Preheat oven to 350°F. For fresh fruit: sprinkle 1 tablespoon sugar over prepared fresh fruit, stir, and set aside to macerate.

2. Lightly oil a 9-inch pie plate or a 2-quart casserole dish. In a bowl combine the milk, eggs, vanilla, 2 tablespoons sugar, flour, salt, and nutmeg. Using a whisk, blend until smooth. It will resemble pancake batter.

3. Spread the fruit in the prepared pie plate. Pour the batter over the top of the fruit. Bake for 30 to 35 minutes, until the top is brown and puffy. Remove from oven and sprinkle with confectioners' sugar. Serve warm.

Applesauce Cake

This is a variation on a cake that was popular in my neighborhood as a kid. Yogurt and applesauce have been added to replace the sour cream and butter that was once used to make this cake moist.

Makes 1 bundt cake, 12 slices; 1 grain/starch per slice; a Sometime choice

1½ cups all-purpose flour
½ cup whole wheat pastry flour
1 teaspoon baking powder
1 teaspoon baking soda
1 teaspoon cinnamon or cardamom
¾ cup granulated sugar
1½ cups plain yogurt
1 teaspoon vanilla extract
2 eggs
½ cup applesauce
Filling
¼ cup granulated sugar
¼ cup wheat germ
1 teaspoon cinnamon

1. Preheat oven to 350°F. Lightly oil a bundt or tube cake pan. Blend together all the dry ingredients.

2. Beat together the yogurt, vanilla, eggs, and applesauce until well combined. Pour over the dry ingredients, gently stirring until all ingredients are moist, but don't overmix. Pour half the batter into the pan. Combine the ingredients for the filling and sprinkle over the batter. Pour the remaining batter over the filling, covering it as best you can.

3. Bake in preheated oven and test for doneness at 30 minutes. A cake tester should come out clean, and the cake should look golden brown. Cook an additional 5 minutes if necessary.

Fruit with Brown Sugar

In the 1980s fresh fruit dipped in soft brown sugar and fresh whipped cream or cool sour cream was a favorite and easy dessert. Today I substitute a good vanilla yogurt for the cream, and the result is just as delicious.

1 cup strawberries equals 1 fruit serving; an Occasional choice

fresh strawberries, tops on
½ cup soft brown sugar
1 cup vanilla or plain yogurt

Wash the strawberries and arrange them on a platter along with the sugar and yogurt. Dip a strawberry halfway into the yogurt then the sugar. Enjoy!

Baked Apples

When I was a kid these were a common fall dessert. The larger apples hold their shape best. Experiment with a variety of apples to see which your family likes best.

Serves 4; 1 fruit

4 large apples
6 tablespoons sugar
4 teaspoons butter (optional)
cinnamon or nutmeg
vanilla frozen yogurt

1. Wash and core the apples. Trim 1 inch of the peel from the top of the apple. Pour 1½ tablespoons of sugar, 1 teaspoon of butter, and a sprinkle of cinnamon or nutmeg in each apple. Place in a baking dish and add approximately 1 inch of water. Bake 30 minutes at 350°F. Baste with the apple juices at 15 minutes.

2. Serve warm topped with a tablespoon of low-fat frozen yogurt.

Blueberry Grunt

I don't know why this dish has this name, but it tastes better than it sounds. It's like eating baked blueberries with a sweetened biscuit on top.

Serves 4; 1½ fruit, 1 grain/starch; a Sometime choice

3 cups blueberries, fresh or frozen
¼ cup sugar
¼ teaspoon cinammon
¼ teaspoon nutmeg
⅓ cup molasses
2 tablespoons lemon juice
½ cup all-purpose flour
½ cup whole wheat pastry flour
1½ teaspoons baking powder
3 tablespoons softened butter
1 tablespoon canola oil
1 egg
⅓ cup milk

1. Preheat oven to 375°F. Wash the berries, removing any stems. In a bowl combine the berries with the sugar, cinnamon, nutmeg, molasses, and lemon juice. Toss lightly until berries are well coated. Pour into a lightly oiled 1-quart baking dish.

2. Combine all the flour with the baking powder and, using a fork or clean fingers, blend in the butter and canola oil. Add the egg and milk and blend until the dough is soft. Drop the dough by spoonfuls onto the berries. Bake for 25 minutes until the crust is golden. Serve hot with vanilla frozen yogurt or ice milk.

Apple Soufflé

This is like eating sweet air—lots of fun for kids.

Serves 4; 1½ fruit; a Sometime choice

6 egg whites
⅓ cup sugar
1 teaspoon vanilla
3 cups applesauce
½ cup coarsely chopped walnuts (optional)

1. Preheat oven to 350°F. Prepare a 1-quart baking or soufflé dish by lightly oiling it with butter and dusting evenly with sugar. Beat the egg whites until they start to thicken and foam. Add the sugar and the vanilla. Beat until firm but not dry. Fold the egg whites gently into the applesauce along with the nuts (if using them). Pour immediately into the prepared baking dish.

2. Bake 20 minutes until lightly brown and firm. Serve with frozen yogurt and a crisp cookie.

Poached Peaches or Pears

Cold fruit makes a perfectly presentable dessert, but my family always prefers a baked fruit over one straight from the refrigerator. This is so easy, and you can even put it together and let it cook while you eat so you have it nice and warm at the end of the meal.

Serves 4; 1 fruit

4 fresh peaches or pears
½ cup sugar
¾ cup water
3 whole cloves

> Peel and halve the fruit. Remove the pit or seeds. Combine the sugar and water and cloves in a saucepan. Bring to a boil. Cook five minutes. Add the fruit. Baste with the sauce and allow to cook until tender (about 15 minutes). Cool in the sauce and serve warm.

Melon Surprise

This is a variation on Baked Alaska. I made it for a family dinner with neighbors, and the kids thought it was lots of fun and good too!

1 large ripe honeydew, Persian, or crenshaw melon
lemon juice
1 quart vanilla, strawberry, or cherry frozen yogurt or ice milk
4 or 5 egg whites
½ cup sugar
chocolate or caramel sauce (optional)

1. Peel the melon carefully. Remove a small wedge and gently scrape all seeds out with a spoon. Slice a thin piece of melon off on the side opposite the wedge. This will keep the melon from rolling around later on. Add a bit of lemon juice to the melon cavity. Chill the melon in the refrigerator at least two hours.

2. Before serving, preheat the oven to 425°F. Beat the egg whites with the sugar until they hold soft peaks. Remove the cold melon and fill with the frozen yogurt. Return the wedge. Set the melon on its flat side on a baking sheet. Quickly frost the entire melon with the meringue. Place in the oven for 8 minutes until the meringue is lightly browned. Remove to a platter with the help of one or two spatulas, and serve at once by cutting slices. You can drizzle with sauce before serving.

Peanut Butter Cupcakes

A cupcake served as an Everyday or Sometime snack needs to be unfrosted or frosted with an icing that is low in fat. This recipe is low in fat, and the cupcakes can be served with or without icing and still taste good. But my kids always prefer them with icing.

Makes 1 dozen; 1 grain/starch; a Sometime choice

½ cup packed brown sugar
¼ cup creamy peanut butter
3 tablespoons softened butter or margarine
1 teaspoon vanilla extract
1 egg
1 cup all-purpose flour
1 teaspoon baking powder
pinch of salt
⅓ cup low-fat milk
icing (optional; recipe follows)

1. Preheat oven to 350°F. Beat the sugar, peanut butter, butter, and vanilla until smooth. Add the egg and blend well.

2. Combine all the dry ingredients and stir with a fork to mix well. Add the dry ingredients to the peanut butter mixture, alternating with the milk, and stir until mixed. Spoon into 12 muffin cups lined with paper liners. Bake for 18 to 20 minutes. Sprinkle with confectioners' sugar or top with Basic Vanilla Frosting (following) or a variation.

Basic Vanilla Icing

Enough to frost 12 cupcakes

1 tablespoon butter
¼ cup granulated sugar
¼ cup low-fat milk
1 to 1½ cups confectioners' sugar
1 teaspoon vanilla extract

Combine the butter and the granulated sugar in a small saucepan. Cook for 1 to 2 minutes on low heat. Remove from heat. Stir in milk and keep stirring until smooth. Slowly add confectioners' sugar and vanilla. Stir until well blended.

Variation: Peanut Butter Frosting

Substitute 1 tablespoon peanut butter for the butter.

Variation: Chocolate Frosting

Replace ¼ cup of the confectioners' sugar with ¼ cup cocoa powder.

Meringue Cookies

These are like little snowflake drops. They carry a fair amount of sugar but absolutely no fat. They can be made ahead and stored in an airtight container and served as a nice accompaniment to baked or poached fruit.

Makes 2 dozen cookies; a sweet/snack/other food choice

4 egg whites
pinch of salt
1 cup sugar
2 teaspoons vanilla

1. Preheat oven to 325°F. Beat egg whites until frothy, then slowly add salt and sugar. Continue beating until the whites hold stiff peaks. Fold in the vanilla.

2. Drop by spoonfuls onto a baking sheet lined with parchment paper. Bake 20 minute until dry and crisp.

Oatmeal Cookies

Oatmeal cookies remain one of my family's favorites. In this recipe some of the butter has been replaced with applesauce to make them lower in fat.

Makes 3 dozen cookies; 3 cookies equal 1 grain/starch; a Sometime choice

1½ cups flour
1 teaspoon baking powder
½ teaspoon cinnamon
½ teaspoon fresh nutmeg (optional)
pinch of salt
¼ cup or ½ stick softened butter or soft margarine
1½ cups brown sugar
¼ cup applesauce
2 eggs
2 teaspoons vanilla
2 to 3 cups oatmeal
1 cup chocolate chips (optional)

1. Preheat oven to 350°F. Combine the flour, baking powder, cinnamon, nutmeg, and salt. Beat the butter with the sugar and applesauce until creamy. Beat in one egg at a time. Stir in vanilla.

2. Stir the flour mixture into the butter mixture. Add the oatmeal and stir until blended. Drop by spoonfuls onto a lightly oiled baking sheet. Bake for 8 minutes.

Chocolate Lovers' Fudge Pudding

Serve this as a Sunday dessert and your family will think it is sinfully rich when it really isn't.

Serves 4; 1½ grain/starch; a Sometime choice

1 cup all-purpose flour
¾ cup granulated sugar
4 tablespoons cocoa powder, unsweetened
2 teaspoons baking powder
⅛ teaspoon salt
½ cup low-fat milk
2 tablespoons melted butter
1 teaspoon vanilla extract
Topping
½ cup dark brown sugar
½ cup granulated sugar
4 tablespoons cocoa powder, unsweetened
1¼ cups water

1. Preheat oven to 350°F. Lightly oil a 1-quart baking dish or a 9-inch cake or pie plate.

2. Sift together the first five ingredients in a medium-size bowl. Add the milk, butter, and vanilla. Stir until well blended. Pour into the prepared pan and set aside.

3. Combine the sugars and cocoa for the topping and sprinkle over the prepared batter. Pour the water over the topping, put do not mix.

4. Bake for 25 to 30 minutes. It should look puffy and a little crispy and be dark brown. Serve hot out of the oven with frozen vanilla yogurt.

Variation: Raspberry Fudge Pudding

Mix 1 cup frozen raspberries into the batter at the end of step 2. Proceed with step 3, but reduce the water to ½ cup. Bake as directed.

9
≡

Questions and Answers

My wife wants to control what our daughter eats, but I think she is making her crazy. I think we can't put too much attention on this or we'll make it worse. You need to tell us what to do.

—FATHER OF AN EIGHT-YEAR-OLD GIRL

I'd say half of my teenagers could actually fit the definition of overweight. They just seem to eat too much and not get enough exercise; and nobody seems to know what to do about it.

—PEDIATRIC NURSE PRACTITIONER

Q. My daughter is overweight, but my husband keeps feeding her doughnuts or cookies whenever they do errands together. I talk to him about this, but he still does it. He says she likes it. What should I do?

A. Sometimes fathers aren't sure how to entertain or interact with their daughters. With a son they can see themselves playing catch or basketball but some men may not think it is okay to "play" or roughhouse with a girl for fear she will get hurt or just not like it. Your husband may have found an activity he and your daughter enjoy, but they need to expand their repertoire. Ask him to do something not related to food, such as playing basketball, woodworking, fishing, taking a walk, even helping with weekend chores. Girls can enjoy these activities just as much as boys, and they will be more athletic if they have encouragement from both parents.

Q. My child is overeating even your Everyday choices. What should I do?

A. Your definition of "overeating" may not really mean he is eating more than he needs. Make sure he is given the opportunity to eat three meals per day along with planned snacks. Your child should also be participating in some form of regular activity such as school recess or an organized sport. Ask your son if he is hungry before he helps himself to a snack or second portions and ask him to eat slowly. The amount of food children need can vary from meal to meal, so if your child is eating because he is truly hungry then he needs to eat. If he is eating out of boredom or anxiety that is another issue.

Q. Desserts are a real battleground in our house. I don't think I should serve dessert if my children haven't finished their meal, but I don't want to force them to eat either.

A. There are several ways you can make dessert a nonissue in your home. One is to prepare desserts that they should be encouraged to eat, such as Baked Apples, page 247, Blackened Bananas, page 240, and Fruit Salad, page 242. These recipes are so packed with nutrition they really are good for your child.

The next time your child is clamoring for a dessert that he knows is coming at the end of a meal, put his dessert portion on a plate next to his dinner plate. Tell him: "Here's your dessert. Eat it whenever you like; I'm having mine at the end of the meal." Let him choose when to eat it. Any child who has ever eaten a frozen dinner has had to decide when to eat his dessert, and from my observation it's usually saved for last. Except for very young children the 300 calories in a serving of dessert will not completely fill him up, and he will still eat at least some of the meal.

Another way to handle the dessert issue is to serve it as often as you are willing to make it from scratch. Years ago the family that wanted a pastry or cake had to make it themselves or buy it at a bakery, usually at a dear price. Today you can buy snack cakes cheaply at every gas station and corner food market. In most homes if you serve sweet snacks or desserts only when you or your child take the time to make them, then the task of preparation makes dessert self-limiting, and the secondary benefits include time together cooking. Dessert does not need to be a part of every meal. It is an enjoyable part of a meal, but it just can't replace the need for nutrition.

Q. I want to teach my children to cook, but all they want to make is dessert. Is this okay?

A. Almost all children will prefer making cupcakes, cake, or cookies over chicken stir-fry or steamed vegetables—it is just more fun. Preparing desserts is a wonderful opportunity to explain why some desserts are not Everyday food choices. For example, on page 199 I deliberately tell parents to teach their children how to prepare a cake from scratch with frosting so you can show your children what goes into a good cake. It requires sugar, butter, cocoa powder, white flour, and eggs. These ingredients are all dense in calories and are not a good way to get nutrition, and for this reason rich desserts like frosted cakes are a Sometime and not an

Everyday food choice. Go ahead and prepare dessert with your children. It will teach them how to cook and make them competent in the kitchen and aware of what goes into food. At around age twelve you can start to encourage a broader selection of recipes.

Q. I am starting my child on a healthier diet, but what do I do about parties? Should I tell her to cut back on the cake or pizza?

A. The occasional party is not what makes any child overweight. Let your child participate in the party just like every other invited child. Do stress sharing food with others and participating in nonfood activities such as games. Do not encourage going back for seconds if other kids haven't had their share—this is a demonstration of good manners, but it keeps food intake down too. You can remind her about manners and good behavior while at the party, but save any talk about what was actually eaten until after the party. Overeating might really be due to hunger and you may want to give her a snack or even a meal before the party.

Q. Should I buy special diet foods?

A. In most cases the answer is no. Some low-fat or diet foods actually carry more calories than regular foods. Diet soda and diet candy confuse children. It tells them it is okay to overeat these foods even when not hungry. It is much better for your child to have real candy or soda and eat it in moderation. The only modified foods encouraged are low-fat calcium choices, such as skim or 1 percent milk, and low-fat protein choices, such as low-fat deli meats. The fat is remove but the essential nutrients are retained.

Q. My child seems always to be hungry and wants to eat sweet foods more than other kids. Why is this?

A. If your child is constantly hungry there could be an underlying medical problem. Check with your doctor. If everything is fine medically, look at how food is handled in the home. When food is being restricted, children can become preoccupied with what they eat. Try to evaluate how your family handles the foods your child is hungry for and make sure he is getting some of the foods he wants, even if they aren't very nutritious. Remember all foods can be served sometimes. The next time you go shopping let your child pick a "sweet" food for which he has been longing. Help him to regulate it himself. Do this by serving the recommended food group servings at meals, but let him have this food as a snack or dessert.

Q. My twelve-year-old son is teased at school. Should I get involved?

A. Don't ignore teasing. If your child is in elementary or middle school you should contact the principle, teacher, or guidance counselor to intervene. Many schools are prepared today with curriculums and workshops that promote respect and acceptance. Teasing is very painful, and you may not be able to stop it, but if you contact the adults responsible for your child at school at least she will see a positive response on your part.

Q. Should I limit food?

A. Limiting food can preoccupy your child with food and even cause overeating or sneaking. Take a more positive approach and make nutritious food more available and fun. Kids love juice boxes, candy, and individually wrapped snacks because the food companies package them so attractively. You may need to do some "marketing" of the Everyday choices yourself by making them more appealing. For example, instead of serving your child a whole orange, make a fruit salad with a variety of colored fruit; or instead of plain crackers, sprinkle low-fat cheese on a whole wheat cracker; add some salsa; and microwave to make a minitaco; or make a small plate of Everyday cookies and fruit wedges for when your child comes home from school; or serve an assortment of beautiful raw vegetables at dinner with your child's favorite salad dressing for dipping.

Q. My husband is so concerned about my daughter's weight that meals have become very stressful. What can I do to change this?

A. People get anxious when they feel out of control. To help your husband and ultimately your daughter you and your husband need to come up with a positive plan of action. The exercises in chapter 7 can accomplish this. Mealtime is not the time to keep track of who is eating what. Meals should be a time to relax and enjoy food. Start with the exercises in chapter 7 and ask your husband to read the truth about diets in chapter 2.

Q. My preteen daughter is counting grams of fat. Is this okay?

A. Label reading can be a great way to learn about nutrition, but in some rare cases it can become obsessive. Make sure your daughter has accurate information about how much fat she needs (look at the suggested levels on page 94). A low-fat diet, which carries about 30 percent of calories from fat, is recommended for almost everyone. Keeping to a low-fat diet is fine, but it is also important for your daughter to get the total calories she needs as well as the recommended servings of all the food groups she needs for her age.

Q. I know I shouldn't check my child's weight, but I really want to know what she should weigh, and so does she. Isn't there a chart I can use?

A. The height and weight of children is so variable it is not easy to say what is "normal." When a child asks "What should I weigh?" and then discovers on a chart that she is above normal, even by only a pound, she will be devastated. As of June 2000, body mass index growth charts can be used to help detect, at an early age, children at risk of being overweight. The body mass index, or BMI, is a formula calculated using height and weight. Tracking a child's BMI through childhood and adolescence is a better indicator of fat mass than height and weight alone.

BMI formula = weight in pounds ÷ height in
inches ÷ height in inches × 703
= BMI.

Children with a BMI greater than the 85th percentile for age are at risk of being overweight. A BMI for age greater than the 95th percentile is considered overweight. To calculate your child's BMI and to find a copy of body mass index for age percentiles for girls and boys, ages two to twenty, go to the U.S. Department of Health and Human Services Web site www.cdc.gov/growthchart. The BMI has been calculated in a nineteen-page table for the full range of height and weight, starting at children weighing as little as 18 pounds and ending at 250 pounds.

Q. My daughter cries and screams when she can't get a food she wants, such as candy or soda. What should I do?

A. Your child will not stop loving you if you don't give in to every request, and habitually giving in will probably set you up for bigger problems later on. Don't ignore the upset child, but try not to acquiesce either. Stay calm and say something such as, "I know you want to have the candy and I know you are disappointed but crying and screaming will not get you what you want. Candy is not something we snack on every day." Young children like rules, so make up a rule to address the candy issue that you can live with. Some families limit candy to one piece per day, others to only hard candy. Others limit candy to gum or holidays like Valentine's Day or Halloween. Set a rule and your child can get mad at the rule, not Mommy—adults have to abide by the rule too.

Q. My three-year-old daughter will not participate in the One-Bite Rule. What should I do?

A. The One-Bite Rule is as important to a child's health as is brushing her teeth, or getting well-child care—it should not be negotiable. Talk about the rule when you are away from the table. Explain to her that eating good food is very important to her health and each time a food is served at the table you will ask her to try one bite. Be firm, clear, and consistent about your rules. Praise her when she does comply, but don't get in a fight at the table. Ultimately, your child controls what goes in her mouth. You will lose if you get in a struggle, but that does not mean you should give up. Keep making the request, and have all family members participate.

Q. I am a very picky eater, yet I want my daughter to eat better than I do. What can I do?

A. Honesty is the best policy. Tell your daughter that you have trouble trying new foods but because you know it is important you too will participate in the One-Bite Rule. It is perfectly okay to let your children know you are not perfect. The point of this rule is to introduce your child to new foods and to support the family identity as one that is willing to try new things.

Q. My husband is a very picky eater and won't try new foods. I think he is part of the reason my son is fussy about food. What should I do?

A. In some cases a parent may not be aware of how children mimic behavior. Ask him if being a picky eater is a trait he would like his child to copy. This at least will call it to his attention. Explain the importance of the One-Bite Rule and ask for his participation.

Q. My four-year-old son just picks at his food. He barely eats, which drives me crazy. Should I make him eat?

A. Children are so picky between the ages of one and five that it is probably a normal part of development. Do not force your child to eat. Continue to offer three meals and serve appropriate snacks and let him eat what he needs. You cannot control what he eats, you can only control what you offer. Remember to watch your language. I hear many parents describe their child as being picky. Try to find something positive about your child's eating habits.

Q. My kids say everybody gets fun snacks at school but them. Can this be true, and what should I do?

A. If your child is feeling left out of the "fun stuff," listen to him—he may have a point. Surprise him with a favorite "fun" snack and then go right back to more nourishing (but in all honesty not as fun), healthier choices. The important element is to listen to your children. I am sure you can distinguish between a casual remark and a genuine concern. Genuine concerns should be addressed. It's all part of thoughtful eating.

Q. At the grocery store my children want me to buy sugar cereal and complain when I don't. Should I buy it?

A. You should have a shopping list with you to avoid impulse buying. It is okay to be flexible when you shop, but some kids will find a food they want in every aisle. Some families set a limit of one unplanned item per trip. This can actually be fun because it can give the kids the chance to try the latest "novelty" food. One spontaneous purchase won't break the nutrition or financial budget. Another way to handle the cereal issue is to serve the heavily sugared cereals as a dessert. When you serve cereal instead of cake or other dessert you teach your child that there is room for all types of food and that these heavily processed foods are more like candy than a real breakfast food. Have them check out the sugar content on the label and compare it to a cookie or a piece of candy. It makes a great dessert that kids really do like.

Q. My child seems to binge eat. Should I limit food?

A. Look at what your child is binging on. Foods in the Sometime and Occasional choices are often foods that may be hard for your child to control on his own. Help your child by keeping mostly Everyday choices in the house and prepare meals and snacks using ingredients from the Everyday choices. Don't eliminate all your Sometime and Occasional choices; try buying half or one-third of what you buy now.

Q. What do I do if I think my child is sneaking food?

A. If your child is sneaking food chances are she already feels guilty about it. Hiding food or locking it up will only make her feel worse. Your daughter could be hungry, in which case she should eat, or if she wants a particular food, find a way for her to have the food and encourage her to eat it in plain sight. Stress that as a family we do things together and that includes eating. Don't set your child up to sneak. Buying favorite foods and "hiding" them can actually teach your child to look for these hidden treats. It's like telling your kids, "I know you'll sneak food if I don't police you"—that puts you in the role of dictator not coach. Try being straightforward. For example, if you buy chocolate cookies for a weekend picnic don't hide them; instead tell everybody not to eat them, because you are saving them for the weekend. Or let them know you bought a box of the family's favorite cookies and want to share them equally. Let your kids know that some foods are expensive and special and that it's just not fair to the rest of the family if one person eats without sharing.

Q. I prepare dinner or lunch and ten minutes later my son wants something to eat. What should I do?

A. If this is turning into a routine, call it to your child's attention. Let him know that you expect him to eat at meals and that after the table is cleared you will not prepare any more food. If he is really hungry allow him to choose from Everyday choices in the vegetable or fruit groups, such as an apple or carrot slices, but keep the choices very limited. If he has not finished his meal, wrap it in plastic and refrigerate it. When he gets hungry he can eat what was left, but only serve it if it is still appetizing. You can't control when kids are hungry, but you don't want them to turn you into a short-order cook either.

Q. My child does not like anything on your Everyday choices for snack foods. Can I give him a food from the Occasional choices?

A. Yes, you can, but the amounts have to be controlled, and this can be difficult. One of the major reasons our children have become overweight is because they like the taste of the foods in the Sometime and Occasional list, and they can't control them as well as they can the Everyday choices. If you buy from the Occasional or Sometimes choices purchase only a small number of these items. The purpose of a snack is to satisfy hunger. If a child is hungry he will eat what is available. Explain to him that you are using nutrition and health to help you in your food selections.

Q. I am worried about my child's weight, but should I bring it up before she does?

A. Chances are if you have noticed your child's weight she has noticed she is bigger than other children her age too. If she asks, "Am I too big?" you can say something like, "You are larger than other children, but because you are a child and still growing, bigger may be normal for you." Kids want reassurance from you that they are okay. Keep the emphasis on eating well and getting the exercise they need.

Q. Should I keep track of my daughter's weight?

A. If you start checking weight the focus is on the scale and not on eating good food and being active. Leave assessing weight to your health care provider, but do practice a healthy lifestyle at home. If you child is talking about weight, pay attention to what family members say about weight. Children hear adults talk about weight all the time at home, on TV, and in magazines. Examine your conversations about weight and look at the magazines you buy. Advertising tells adults we are not okay the way we are, and it presents unrealistic ideals for children. Select magazines that carry ads using people of all different sizes or review a magazine with your child and point out how perfect the models look. The next time you are at the mall or other group gathering place, ask your child how many of the people look "perfect." This will help her see how unrealistic the ideal body image promoted in the media really is.

Q. On the Real Food Diet I feel like I am depriving my child of eating fun food. Am I?

A. It may feel unnatural to have no or very few processed or ready-to-eat snack foods around at first, but if you observe how it helps your child self-regulate then you will see that it is the right thing to do. You are not depriving your child, you are protecting her.

Q. My son is a vegetarian. Is this okay?

A. Vegetarian eating can be a very healthy way of eating. In most cases a well-planned vegetarian menu can be quite healthy and may reduce the risk for some cancers and heart disease. But just being vegetarian alone does not ensure good nutrition or weight loss. I have met vegetarians who eat no animal products but eat a steady diet of potato chips, snack cakes, and macaroni and cheese with few vegetables. And eliminating entire food groups from a child's menu does require more thoughtful menu planning. A child who eats nothing but fruits, vegetables, grains, legumes, seeds, and nuts will be eating foods very high in fiber and bulk and such a menu may cause a child to feel full before he has met his need for energy.

If your child is a pure vegan, that is, he eats no meat, milk, or eggs, you should speak to a professional knowledgeable in planning such diets. It is critical your child get the nutrition needed for growth.

Protein is the nutrient parents worry about most when a child is on a vegetarian diet, but perhaps unnecessarily. See page 95 to determine how much protein your child requires—the range is 16 to 59 grams, depending on age and sex. Protein can be obtained from many nonanimal sources. Each serving from the grain group carries at least 2 grams of protein, and this adds up very quickly. Nonmeat sources from the protein group such as beans, soybeans, nuts, and nut butters are effective ways to obtain protein, carrying 8 grams or more protein each serving. If your child drinks milk or eats cheese, each serving can supply 8 grams of protein too. Soy milk is a good protein source as well. The vegetable group carries small but measurable amounts of protein that provide about 1 gram in each ½ cup. The child that eats a little from all the essential food groups over the course of a day will meet his needs for protein.

When meat, dairy, or animal products are eliminated, good sources of calcium, iron, zinc, vitamin B12, and vitamin D are reduced too. A recent position paper by the American Dietetic Association suggested that docosahexaenoic acid (DHA) a fatty acid important to health, may be low when not eating fish or eggs.

Calcium deficiencies are rare in vegetarians and will probably be even less of a problem with the growing number of calcium-fortified foods available to us such as juice and cereals. Vegetarians may absorb and retain more calcium from food than do nonvegetarians because higher protein intake is associated with a lower level of calcium retention.

Good vegetarian sources of calcium include: legumes (1 cup cooked provides 80 to 125 mg), soy foods (½ cup tofu, 120 to 350 mg; 1 cup fortified soy milk, 250 to 300 mg), nuts and seeds (2 tbsp, 60 mg), green leafy vegetables (½ cup cooked, 75 to 180 mg), fortified orange juice (1 cup calcium-fortified, 300 mg).

Iron is an extremely important nutrient for all children, and iron deficiency anemia is the most common nutrition deficiency among children. Despite the fact that the iron found in animal products is better absorbed than the form contained in vegetables and grains, the level of iron deficiency anemia in vegetarians is similar to the rate found in nonvegetarians. It may be that vegetarians consume greater amounts of vitamin C–rich foods, such as citrus fruit, which aids iron absorption, thus preventing the problem.

Good vegetarian sources of iron include: bran flakes (1 cup, 11 mg), sea vegetables (½ cup cooked, 18 to 42 mg), tofu (½ cup, 6.6 mg), nuts and seeds (2 tbsp, 1 to 2.5 mg).

Zinc is important for your child's growth and development. Zinc is plentiful in animal products, but most vegetarians have adequate zinc levels.

Good vegetarian sources of zinc include: bran flakes (1 cup, 5 mg), wheat germ (2 tbsp, 2.3 mg), legumes (½ cup cooked, 1 mg), soy foods (½ cup cooked soybeans, tempeh, tofu, textured vegetable protein, 1 to 1.5 mg), dairy foods (1 cup milk or yogurt, 1 to 1.8 mg; 1 ounce cheddar cheese, 0.9 mg).

The amount of B12 we need is minuscule but extremely important. B12 is found in all animal products. If your child's menu includes milk/cheese or eggs he should obtain the B12 he needs. If he is a vegan he must get a reliable source to prevent a deficiency that will occur over time in a chronically deficient diet. Spirulina, seaweed, tempeh, and other fermented foods are not reliable sources of B12. Good vegetarian sources of vitamin B12 include: vitamin supplements, fortified breakfast cereals (1.5 to 6.0 mcg per ¾ cup), meat analogs (1 serving, 2.0 to 7.0 mcg) and fortified soy beverages (1 cup, 0.2 to 5.0

mcg), nutritional yeast (Red Star Vegetarian Support Formula 1 tbsp, 4.0 mcg).

Vitamin D is easily obtained in fortified milk. Children who follow a vegan or veganlike diet must obtain a reliable source of vitamin D. Sunlight can be that source if the child has regular sun exposure, but children living in the northern climates where sun exposure is limited must get a dietary source.

Good vegetarian sources include: fortified ready-to-eat cereal (¾ cup, 1.0 to 2.5 mcg), fortified soy milk or other nondairy milk (1 cup, 1.0 to 2.5 mcg).

Diets that do not include fish or eggs will lack the fatty acid DHA (docosahexaeonic acid), which may be beneficial to our health by keeping cholesterol levels normal and blood healthy. Foods rich in linolenic acid, an essential fatty acid that can convert to DHA in the body, should be included in a vegetarian menu to obtain the potential health benefits DHA can provide. Good vegetarian sources of DHA include: flaxseed; walnuts; oils: walnut, canola, linseed, soybean; and cooked soybeans and tofu.

Q. Should my child take supplements?

A. Each week we read fascinating headlines about the benefits of nutrients in disease prevention and treatment. So what parent wouldn't think extra nutrients, in the form of supplements, is a good idea? It is hard to say how many children take supplements, but according to the *Nutrition Business Journal* supplement sales in 1998 reached 13.9 billion dollars, and a spokesperson at the Council for Responsible Nutrition estimates half of all parents give their children supplements. Is supplementing your child's diet a good idea, and if yes, with what?

According to the American Dietetic Association, eating a wide variety of foods is the best way for children to get their nutrition. The American Academy of Pediatrics in its *Pediatric Nutrition Handbook* writes that nutrition surveys have found little evidence of vitamin and mineral inadequacies (except for iron) in our children and therefore have not recommended routine supplementation in healthy children. Supplements are needed for specific childhood illnesses such as cystic fibrosis, inflammatory bowel disease, and some forms of liver disease. Multivitamins and minerals may be appropriate for children and adolescents with "anorexia or poor and capricious appetites, or those consuming fad diets." The Real Food Diet advocated in this book will provide children with all the nutrition they need. However, despite the absence of an endorsement for supplements, many parents still perceive supplements as dietary insurance, a means to provide a safety net for any nutrients that might be missing in a picky eater's diet. If your child is not a robust vegetable eater, or he can't find a fruit that appeals to him, or he turns down iron-rich food such as meat or legumes, or he doesn't like whole wheat bread as much as white bread, you may want to give your child a multi-vitamin-mineral too. If you do, choose a supplement that will do no harm.

There is little evidence that low-dose multi-vitamin-mineral preparations cause harm, and for that reason pediatricians and nutritionists recommend the use of multi-vitamins-minerals to children and not the use of single-dose nutrients. Given in excess, many nutrients work against each other or can be stored until they reach toxic levels. A child who is given single-dose nutrients may be at greater risk of toxicity because of his size. Even nutrients that are essential to our survival can become harmful: vitamin A taken in excess can be toxic, too much vitamin E interferes with vitamin K, large doses of calcium interfere with iron absorption, and zinc supplementation can interfere with copper, impair the immune system, and decrease "good" cholesterol levels. Unless your health care provider has prescribed a specific supplement, such as iron, the best course for parents is to select a multi-vitamin-mineral supplement that comes closest to meeting the percent DV listed on the label. The percent DV (daily value) is the new label term for the percentage of the reference daily intake for each nutrient. (See box, Nutrition Labeling of Dietary Supplements, page 277.) The reference daily intake is the term being used to replace recommended dietary allowances. Such a product will be the most effective at rounding out your child's nutrient intake.

Don't be lured by labels that say "high potency," "extra B vitamins," "extra vitamin C," or "fortified with herbs." "High potency" means that two of the nutrients it contains have at least 100 percent of the DV, and such a claim can apply to almost all multivitamins, making the term meaningless in most cases. Your child does not need extra B vitamins (which are cheap and probably added only as a marketing ploy) or vitamin C or iron (unless your doctor says so), and bits of herbs only increase the cost. Where you buy your supplements does not matter either, according to the Center for Science in the Public interest, because most vitamin companies buy their nutrients from the same few manufacturers. The inclusion of "natural" or "chelated" on the label makes little if any difference and may increase the cost. A thirty-day supply of multivitamins can cost as little as one to four dollars a month. Search out the less expensive store brands, which often replicate the fancier, heavily advertised supplements.

Do look for supplements that contain both minerals and vitamins but don't avoid the multi-vitamins-minerals that do not meet 100 percent DV for all nutrients; putting 100 percent of the DV for calcium in one tablet for example, would make it too big, and since calcium is easy to get in dairy food and fortified juice, most kids do not need to get all their calcium from pills. Children's multi-vitamin-mineral preparations often carry the same nutrients as the adult products but they are chewable and most kids like these better. Remember too that your child must get most of his nutrition from food and that the supplement is just insurance and not a food substitute.

NUTRITION LABELING OF DIETARY SUPPLEMENTS FOR ADULTS AND CHILDREN FOUR OR OLDER

This information will appear on labels along with the percent (%) of the daily value (DV) supplied in each dose.

vitamin A	5,000 IU
vitamin C	60 mg
calcium	1.0 g
iron	18 mg

vitamin D	400 IU
vitamin E	30 IU
vitamin K	80 mcg
thiamin	1.5 mg
riboflavin	1.7 mg
niacin	20 mg
vitamin B6	2.0 mg
folate	0.4 mg
vitamin B12	6.0 mcg
biotin	0.3 mg
pantothenic acid	10 mg
phosphorous	1.0 g
iodine	150 mcg
magnesium	400 mg
zinc	15 mg
selenium	70 mcg
copper	2 mg
manganese	2 mg
chromium	120 mcg
molybdenum	75 mcg
chloride	3400 mg

NUTRITION LABELING FOR DIETARY SUPPLEMENTS FOR INFANTS AND CHILDREN UNDER FOUR

According to the FDA, these daily values (DV) are to be used for labeling products for use by infants and young children. If a nutrient is included for which there is no reference value, the nutrient should carry a footnote that states "daily value not established."

Nutrient	Infant	Child under 4
vitamin A	1,500 IU	2,500 IU
vitamin D	400 IU	400 IU
vitamin E	5 IU	10 IU
vitamin C	35 mg	40 mg
folic acid	0.1 mg	0.2 mg
thiamin	0.5 mg	0.7 mg
riboflavin	0.6 mg	0.8 mg
niacin	8 mg	9 mg
vitamin B6	0.4 mg	0.7 mg
vitamin B12	2 mcg	3 mcg
biotin	.05 mg	.15 mg
pantothenic acid	3 mg	5 mg
calcium	.6 g	.8 g
phosphorous	.5 g	.8 g

iodine	45 mcg	70 mcg
iron	15 mg	10 mg
magnesium	70 mg	200 mg
copper	0.6 mg	1.0 mg
zinc	5 mg	8 mg

References

General References

Modern Nutrition in Health and Disease. 8th ed. Philadelphia: Lea and Febiger, 1993.

Modern Nutrition in Health and Disease. 9th ed. Baltimore: Williams and Wilkins, 1999.

American Academy of Pediatrics Committee on Nutrition. *Pediatric Nutrition Handbook.* 3rd ed. Elk Grove Village, IL: American Academy of Pediatrics, 1993.

Pennington, J. A. *Bowes and Church's Food Values of Portions Commonly Used.* 17th ed. Philadelphia: Lippincott, 1998.

Barlow, S. E. Electronic Article: "Obesity Evaluation and Treatment: Expert Committee Recommendations." *Pediatrics* 102, no. 3 (September 1998). URL: http://www.pediatrics.org/cgi/content/full/102/3/e29.

Epstein, L. H. "Treatment of Pediatric Obesity." *Pediatrics* 101 (March 1998):554–70.

Introduction

Talking with Teens: The YMCA Parent and Teen Survey Final Report. URL: http:www.ymca.net/presrm/ research/ teensurvey.htm

White House Council of Economic Advisers. "Teens and Their Parents in the Twenty-first Century: An Examination of Trends in Teen Behavior and the Role of Parental Involvement." URL: gov/wh/eop/cea/html/teens_paper_final.pdf.

Chapter 1

Dietz, William H. "Health Consequences of Obesity in Youth: Chidhood Predictors of Adult Disease." *Pediatrics* 101 (supplement) (March 1998): 518–25.

Gidding, Samual S. "Understanding Obesity in Youth AHA Medical/Scientific Statement." *Circulation* 94 (December 15, 1996): 3383–87.

"Kids Overweight Influenced by Parents BMI and Family Income." *Journal of the American Dietetic Association* 9 (August 1999): 914.

Mokdad, A. H. "The Spread of the Obesity Epidemic in the United States." 1991–1998 *Journal of the American Medical Association* 282 (October 27, 1999): 1519–22.

Moran, Rebecca. "Evaluation and Treatment of Childhood Obesity." *American Family Physician* 59 (February 15, 1999): 861–68.

Munoz, Kathryn A. "Food Intakes of US Children and Adolescents Compared with Recommendations." *Pediatrics* 100 (September 1997): 323–29.

"Predictors of Obesity in Children." *Obesity Research* 2, no. 6 (November 1994): 579.

Pugliese, Michael T. "Parental health beliefs as a cause of nonorganic failure to thrive." *Pediatrics* 80 (1987): 175–82.

Robertson, S. M. "Factors Related to Addiposity Among Children Aged 3 to 7 Years." *Journal of the American Dietetic Association* 99 (August 1999): 938–43.

Rosenbaum, Michael. "The Physiology of Body Weight Regulation: Relevance to the Etiology of Obesity in Children." *Pediatrics* 101 (supplement) (March 1998): 525–39.

Sanchez, Rene. "Industry Tries to Fit Wider Americans." *Boston Sunday Globe* (April 25, 1999): A9.

Strong, Jack P. "Prevalence and Extent of Atherosclerosis in Adolescents and Young Adults." *Journal of the American Medical Association* 281 (February 24, 1999):727–35.

Styne, Dennis M. "Childhood Obesity: Time for Action, Not Complacency." *American Family Physician* 59 (February 15, 1999): 758–61, 762.

Chapter 2

Epstein, L. H. "Treatment of Pediatric Obesity." *Pediatrics* 101 (1998): 554–70.

Foreman, Judy. "Study Links Parental Bond to Teenage Well-being." *Boston Globe* (September 10, 1997): A01.

Foreyt, J. P. and Goodrick, G. K. "Weight Management Without Dieting." *Nutrition Today* (March/April 1993): 4–9.

Fraser, L. "The Diet Trap." *The Family Therapy Networker* (May/June 1997): 45–52, 67.

Schreiber, G. B. "Weight Modification Efforts Reported by Black and White Preadolescent Girls: National Heart, Lung, and Blood Institute Growth and Health Study." *Pediatrics* 98 (July 1996): 63–70.

Trowbridge, F. "Measuring Dietary Behaviors Among Adolescents." *Public Health Reports* 108 (supplement 1) (1993): 37–41.

Chapter 3

Birch, L. "Development of Eating Behaviors Among Children and Adolescents." *Pediatrics* 101 (March 1998): 539–49.

———. "The Variability of Young Children's Energy Intake." *New England Journal of Medicine* 324 (1991): 232–35.

Evers, C. "Empower Children to Develop Healthful Eating Habits." *Journal of the American Dietetic Association* 97 (supplement 2) (October 1997): S116.

Field, A. "Exposure to the Mass Media and Weight Concerns Among Girls." Electronic abstracts. *Pediatrics* 103, no. 3. URL: http://www.pediatrics.org/cgi/content/full/103/3/e36.

Meltz, B. F. "Mommy I'm Fat." *Boston Globe* (January 16, 1997): F1.

Satter, E. "The Feeding Relationship: Problems and Interventions." *The Journal of Pediatrics* 117 (August 1990): S181–89.

———. "Internal Regulation and the Evolution of Normal Growth as the Basis for Prevention of Obesity in Children." *Journal of the American Dietetic Association* 96 (September 1996): 860–64.

White House Council of Economic Advisers. "Teens and Their Parents in the Twenty-first Century: An Examination of Trends in Teen Behavior and the Role of Parental Involvement." URL: gov/wh/eop/cea/html/teens_paper_final.pdf.

Chapter 4

Anderson, Bob. *Stretching*. Volinas, California Shelter Pub-
lications. 1980.

Dietary Guidelines for Americans. URL: www.health.gov/
dietaryguidelines.

"Improving Children's Health Through Physical Activity:
A New Opportunity. A Survey of Parents and Children about Physical Activity Patterns." Executive
summary, July 1997. International Life Sciences Institute, Washington, D.C.

Klesges, R. C. "A Longitudinal Analysis of Accelerated
Weight Gain in Preschool Children." *Pediatrics* 95
(January 1995): 126–30.

Kohl, H. W. "Development of Physical Activity Behaviors
Among Children and Adolescents." *Pediatrics* 101
(March 1998): 549–54.

Kong, D. "Exercise Seen Boosting Children's Brain Func-
tion." *Boston Globe* (November 9, 1999): A1.

1996 Surgeon General's Report on Physical Activity and
Health. Executive summary, Superintendent of Docu-
ments, Pittsburgh, PA.

Chapter 5

"Are You Eating Right?" *Consumer Reports* (October 1992).

Critser, Greg. "Let Them Eat Fat." *Harper's Magazine*
(March 2000) 41–47.

CSPI Year 2000 Report. Center for Science in the Public
Interest, 1875 Connecticut Ave., N.W., Suite 300,
Washington, D.C. 20009-5728.

Dennison, B. A. "Excess Fruit Juice Consumption by Pre-School-Aged Children Is Associated with Short Stature and Obesity." *Pediatrics* 99, no. 1 (January 1997): 15–22.

"Drink Yourself Fat." *Nutrition Action Health Letter* (April 1999): 11.

Foster-Powell, K. "International Tables of Glycemic Index." *American Journal of Clinical Nutrition* 62 (1995): 871S–93S.

Kimm, S. Y. "The Role of Dietary Fiber in the Development and Treatment of Childhood Obesity." *Pediatrics* 96 (November 1995): 1010–14.

Lampe, J. "Health Effects of Vegetables and Fruit: Assessing Mechanisms of Action in Human Experimental Studies." *American Journal of Clinical Nutrition* 70 (supplement) (September 1999): 475S–90S.

Liebman, B. "Sugar, the Sweetening of the American Diet." *Nutrition Action Health Letter.* (November 1998): 3–8.

Ludwig, D. S. "Dietary Fiber, Weight Gain, and Cardiovascular Disease Risk Factors in Young Adults." *Journal of the American Medical Association* 282 (October 27, 1999): 1539–46.

———. "High Glycemic Index Foods, Overeating, and Obesity." Electronic Article: *Pediatrics* 103, no. 3 (March 1999): e26. URL: http://www.pediatrics.org/cgi/content/full/103/3/e26.

Modern Nutrition in Health and Disease. 8th ed. IBID p. 765.

Mokdad, A. H. "The Spread of the Obesity Epidemic in the United States." 1991–1998 *Journal of the American Medical Association* 282 (October 27, 1999): 1519–22.

Munoz, K. "Food Intakes of US Children and Adolescents Compared with Recommendations." *Pediatrics* 100 (September 1997): 323–29.

Pediatric Nutrition Surveillance 1997. Full Report. Centers for Disease Control and Prevention. Atlanta: U.S. Department of Health and Human Services, Centers for Disease Control, 1998.

Rimm, E. B. "Vegetable, Fruit and Cereal Fiber Intake and Risk of Coronary Heart Disease Among Men." *Journal of the American Medical Association* 275, no. 6 (February 14, 1996): 447–51.

Salmeron, J. "Dietary Fiber, Glycemic Load, and Risk of Non-Insulin-Dependent Diabetes Mellitus in Women." *Journal of the American Medical Association* 277, no. 6 (February 12, 1997): 472–77.

Saltus, R. "Lifestyle Seen As Key to Cancer Prevention." *Boston Globe* (December 11, 1997): A34.

Skinner, J. D. "Fruit Juice Intake Not Related to Children's Growth." *Pediatrics* 103, no. 1 (January 1999): 58–64.

Slavin, J. L. "Plausible Mechanisms for the Protectiveness of Whole Grains." *American Journal of Clinical Nutrition* 70 (supplement) (September 1999): 459S–63S.

Weiland, S. K. "Intake of Trans Fatty Acids and Prevalence of Childhood Asthma and Allergies in Europe." *Lancet* 353, no. 9169 (June 12, 1999): 2040–41.

Wolk, A. "Long-Term Intake of Dietary Fiber and Decreased Risk of Coronary Heart Disease Among Women." *Journal of the American Medical Association* 281 (June 2, 1999): 1998–2004.

Wootan, M. "Trans: the Phantom Fat." *Nutrition Action Health Letter* (September 1996): 10–13.

Chapter 6

"Everyday, Sometimes and Occasional Foods." *Team Nutritions Teacher Handbook*. Food and Consumer Service, U.S. Department of Agriculture, 1997.

Rolls, B. J. "Serving Portion Size Influences 5-Year-Old but Not 3-Year-Old Children's Food Intake." *Journal of the American Dietetic Association* 100, no. 2 (February 2000): 232–34.

Talking with Teens: The YMCA Parent and Teen Survey. Final report. URL: http://www.ymca.net/presrm/research/Δteensurvey.htm.

Chapter 7

"Child Obesity Tied to Television, Playtime Habits." *Boston Globe* (March 25, 1998):A1.

Epstein, H. "Ten-Year Follow-up of Behavioral, Family-Based Treatment for Obese Children." *Journal of the American Medical Association* 264, no. 19 (November 21, 1990): 2519–23.

Flodmark, E. "Prevention of Progression to Severe Obesity in a Group of Obese Schoolchildren Treated with Family Therapy." *Pediatrics* 91, no. 5 (May 1993): 880–84.

"Food Advertisements on Children's Television." *American Family Phsyician* 52, no. 5 (October 1995): 1522–24.

Gortmaker, S. L. "Television Viewing As a Cause of Increasing Obesity Among Children in the United

States 1986–1990." *Archives of Pediatrics and Adolescent Medicine* 150, no. 4 (April 1996) 356–62.

Kosharek, Susan. *If Your Child Is Overweight: A Guide for Parents.* Chicago: American Dietetic Association, 1993.

Mackenzie, Margaret. "Is the Family Meal Disappearing?" *The Journal of Gastronomy* (Winter/Spring 1993): 35–45.

Munoz, Kathryn A. "Food Intakes of US Children and Adolescents Compared with Recommendations." *Pediatrics* 100 (September 1997): 323–29.

Neumark-Sztainer, D. "Factors Influencing Food Choices of Adolescents: Findings from Focus-Group Discussions with Adolescents." *Journal of the American Dietetic Association* 99 (August 1999) 929–34, 937.

Talking with Teens: The YMCA Parent and Teen Survey. Final report. URL: http://www.ymca.net/presrm/research/teensurvey.htm.

Chapter 8

Colwin, Laurie. "Feeding Your Critter." *The Journal of Gastronomy* 7, no. 1 (Winter/Spring 1993): 27–33.

Sykes Wylie, Mary. "Our Trip to Bountiful." *The Family Networker* (May/June 1997): 23–33, 66.

Chapter 9

Liebman, Bonnie. "Multiple Choice: How to Pick a Multivitamin." *Nutrition Action Health Letter* 27, no. 3 (April 2000): 5–13

"Position of the American Dietetic Association: Vegetarian Diets." *Journal of the American Dietetic Association* 97 (November 1997): 1317–21.

"Position of the American Dietetic Association: Vitamin and Mineral Supplementation." *Journal of the American Dietetic Association* 96 (January 1996): 73–77.

Sarubin, Allison. *The Health Professional's Guide to Popular Dietary Supplements.* American Dietetic Association, 2000. Published in United States of America.

Resources

The following are general information sources about
food, nutrition, and children's health.

Food and Health Web Sites

American Academy of Pediatrics
http://www.aap.org

Fast Food Information
Cyberdiet.com

International Food Information Council (IFIC)
http://ificinfo.health.org/

KidsHealth
http://KidsHealth.org

General Health Information
www.usda.gov/cnpp/insights.htm
http//www.cdc.gov/health/diseases.htm

Department of Health and Human Services
Healthfinder
www.healthfinder.gov

Health on the Net Foundation
www.hon.ch

National Council Against Health Fraud, Inc.
www.ncahf.org

National Institutes of Health
    www.nih.gov

PubMed National Library of Medicine
    www.ncbi.nlm.nih.gov/pubmed/

Tufts Nutrition Navigator
    www.navigator.tufts.edu

Weight Control and Obesity Information Sources
    WIN Weight Loss Information Network
    This organization provides the latest science-based
    information on obesity, weight control, and nutrition
    disorders.
        WIN 1 WIN Way
        Bethesda, MD 20892-3665; 301-984-7378.
        http://www.niddk.nih.gov

Shapedown Pediatric Obesity Program
    A national hospital-based family outpatient program
    for the treatment of childhood obesity.
        11 Library Place
        San Anselmo, CA 94960; 415-453-8886
        or 888-724-5245

Eating Disorders
    American Anorexia/Bulemia Association, Inc.
    418 East Seventy-sixth Street
    New York, NY 10021
    212-575-6200

    Anorexia Nervosa and Related Eating Disorders, Inc.
    P.O. Box 5102
    Eugene, OR 97405
    503-344-1144

Vegetarianism
 American Dietetic Association
 216 W. Jackson Boulevard, Suite 800
 Chicago, IL 60606-6995
 1-800-877-1600
 www.eatright.org

REAL FOOD SCIENCE

What we eat effects our health as well as the weight of our children. Most Americans obtain information about nutrition from television and magazines, and only 11 percent identify their physician as a nutrition resource. To prevent disease and obesity it is essential for all health care providers to talk to their patients about what they eat. To make this task easier I have created the web site *realfoodscience.com*. The purpose of this site is to provide health professionals with accurate, reliable nutrition resources with the long-range goal of integrating nutrition education into every medical practice. Health care providers will find nutrition education fact sheets that can be downloaded free-of-charge and reproduced as needed. Please inform your health care provider about this web site. Thank you.

Eileen Behan, RD

Index

involvement in child's eating, 90–92
as primary teachers, 30
restricting food, 19
too-relaxed, 34, 44, 45, 49–51
Parties, 261
Pasta and sauce meal, 189
Pastas/rice, shopping for, 186
Pediatric Nutrition Handbook, 275
Pediatrics (journal), 15, 26, 36, 74, 76, 79, 81, 176
Percent DV (daily value), 276, 277–78, 279–80
Phosphorus, 109
Physical education, 59, 63
Physical exam, 7
Physical issues in dieting, 21
Phytochemicals, 70, 72, 77
Picky eaters, 266–67
Pipher, Mary, xi
Pizza, 191
recipes, 224, 226
Plan of action, 47, 151, 174–75, 263
exercise, 64
individual, 176
living, 177–78
Play, 62, 63, 168
Portions, 143
see also Serving size
Potassium, 109
Potatoes, 121, 190
recipe, 234
steak and, 193

Poultry, 126
everyday choices, 127–28
occasional choices, 129
shopping for, 184
sometime choices, 128
Prepared foods
not mentioned in food groups, 187–89
Prepubescent growth (plumpness), 6
Prevention (magazine), 27
Processed foods, 71, 72, 75, 91
Produce, fresh, 183
Prohibition, 36, 37
Protein, 95, 108, 116
in vegetarian diet, 271–72
Protein group, 99, 102, 105, 107, 126–29, 146, 152, 189
nonmeat sources, 272
nutrients in, 111
substitutions, 196
Protecting children, 39, 271
Psychological issues, 7
Puberty, age of, 2–3
Pudding
recipes, 241, 256–57
Pugliese, Michael T., 19
Punishment, food as, 51, 52, 53, 166
Pyridoxine, 109

Real food, 69–89, 91, 146
cooking, 181–257
defined, 70
health benefits in, 73–74